Wisconsin

Wisconsin

Compiled and edited by Jill Weber Dean
With an introduction by Clay Schoenfeld

Wisconsin Trails/Tamarack Press
P.O. Box 5650
Madison, Wisconsin 53705

Near Rainbow Flowage, in Oneida County—
Robert McQuilkin

Library of Congress Cataloging in Publication Data
Main entry under title:

Wisconsin.

    1. Wisconsin—Description and travel—1951-
—Views. I. Dean, Jill.
F582.W57   917.75'04'4   78-15753
ISBN 0-915024-17-9

Designed by Phill Thill Design.

Typeset by Parkwood Composition
Service, Incorporated.

Printed in the United States of America
by Litho Productions, Incorporated.

First printing 1978

Contents

Introduction   **6**

Spring   **17**

including selections by
August Derleth
Roger Drayna
Steve Hopkins
Justin Isherwood
Aldo Leopold
Michael O'Malley
Larry Van Goethem
Digby B. Whitman

Summer   **53**

including selections by
John Burroughs
Mel Ellis
Robert and Maryo Gard
Aldo Leopold
John Muir
Jay Scriba
Larry Van Goethem

Autumn   **91**

including selections by
Phil Carspecken
Vernon Carstensen
Raymond Helminiak
Dion Henderson
Aldo Leopold
Clay Schoenfeld
Larry Van Goethem

Winter   **125**

including selections by
Charles C. Bradley
August Derleth
Fred L. Holmes
Richard Mc Cabe
Camille Pisani
Jay Scriba
George Vukelich
Robert W. Wells
David Wood

Credits   **160**

Introduction

You can find Wisconsin in many things.

You can find Wisconsin in her diverse cultural heritage. The Erie Canal opened in 1825 and channeled the first flood of immigration to Wisconsin. Up the Hudson River from New York's harbor, through the Erie Canal, and across the Great Lakes to Milwaukee, Racine, Kenosha—that was the route. A reporter stood on the Milwaukee docks in 1843 and wrote: "The torrent of immigration swells very strongly. . . .The refugees arrive daily in their national dresses. . . .Here, on the pier, I see disembarking the Germans, the Norwegians, the Swedes, the Swiss, the Irish." Other nationalities soon joined the flood. Today their descendants and the descendants of Wisconsin's first residents—American Indians—lend a proud richness to the state.

You can find Wisconsin in her greatest natural resource—her people. In 1873 Judge Edward G. Ryan addressed a University of Wisconsin assembly. In the audience was a young man for whom the speech was a turning point in a remarkable career. The magic name: Robert Marion La Follette. Belle Case La Follette joined her husband on the stump to inveigh against the special interests then holding the Wisconsin legislature hostage. With consistent high ideals and actions, "Old Bob" dominated thirty years of Wisconsin history and made his mark on national politics as well.

But in a state known for progressive traditions, La Follette was just another Progressive. Before him, Dr. William Beaumont's discoveries about the digestive process—carried on at army forts in the Wisconsin wilderness—brought important advances to medicine. Two days after Increase Lapham landed in Milwaukee, in 1836, he made the first of the botanical and geological studies that were to lay the basis of Wisconsin's ecological knowledge. Michael Frank—Kenosha newspaper editor and territorial legislator—led the campaign for one of the first free public schools outside New England. Carl Schurz's political career in Wisconsin was climaxed in Washington in a pioneer defense of American Indians and American forests. Five Ringling brothers put together "the Greatest Show on Earth." Carrie Jacobs Bond composed the lyrics that made her "the unpretentious wild rose" of songdom. Lorraine Hansberry wrote *Raisin in the Sun,* the prizewinning play about "people, Negroes, and life." Frank Lloyd Wright created some of the most striking buildings of the modern world. Georgia O'Keeffe originated a form of painting that renewed art in America. Vince Lombardi's Packers made Green Bay "Titletown, U.S.A." And Henry Aaron, who had broken into the major leagues in Wisconsin, helped the Milwaukee Braves win two pennants and a World Series while he became America's home-run king, surpassing even the unsurpassable Babe Ruth.

"There is a special place in my heart for Milwaukee," Aaron said, "and for the special people of Wisconsin."

At Old World Wisconsin, an outdoor museum of ethnic architecture, in Waukesha County near Eagle—Jeff Dean

You can find Wisconsin in her magnificent farmland—sprawling homesteads, rugged red barns, spotless milk houses. Even if you didn't see the auto license plates stamped America's Dairyland, you'd know you were in an agricultural heartland. Drive out of any city in the state, and within minutes you'll be in farming country. Holsteins graze in grassy pastures, arrow-straight rows of golden oats and dark green corn bend with the breeze, and J. I. Case tractors chug over the fields. Wisconsin no longer has more cows than people—a distinction we surrendered long ago—but it still has more dairy cattle than any other state in the nation. These cows give Wisconsin first rank in milk and cheese production, and keep the state among the top three in nearly all other dairy products.

To a pioneer farm-woman goes credit for starting Wisconsin on its way to dairying leadership. Back in about 1840 Armine Pickett arrived from the East with a few cows. Wheat-growing dominated Wisconsin agriculture at the time, and though Pickett saw promise for dairying in the wild grasses flourishing in Jefferson County, he didn't know how to produce butter and cheese on a commercial scale without a lot of cows. His wife, Ann, had the answer. "We have ten cows and between our neighbors I can count up ten more. Let's pool our milk," she proposed, "and I will make it into cheese right here in our kitchen."

The Picketts were followed by innovators like Chester Hazen and William Dempster Hoard, who championed dairying as Wisconsin's wheat boom died out. The transition was completed when, at Philadelphia's Centennial Exhibition of 1876, dairy products from Wisconsin won more medals than those from any other state. We've never been headed since.

You can find Wisconsin in her seas of green forests, though it wasn't always so. For a dramatic era, the lumber barons bestrode Wisconsin in the boots of Paul Bunyan. We know them now for the names they left on maps, public buildings, and whole institutions: Washburn, Woodman, Knapp, Stout, Sawyer, Stephenson, Spooner, Weyerhaeuser, Vilas. With their lumberjacks, they cut the forests. As one of them said, in the philosophy of the day, "If God had not meant Wisconsin's pineries to be cut to build Chicago, he would not have caused the rivers of the state to flow southward."

Nature, too, took a toll. Wisconsin's worst disaster, and one of the worst in history, was the fire that swept Peshtigo in 1871. All northeastern Wisconsin was a howling hell of flames, and the death count was five times higher than that from the Chicago fire, which took place on the same night. But today Wisconsin is green again, thanks to farsighted reforestation laws and a new breed of lumberman, the professional forester.

9

Holsteins on a Richland County farm—
Phil McCafferty

You can find Wisconsin in her cities and small towns. The gateway to Wisconsin was—and is—through the ports of the Great Lakes. On the shores of these dramatic inland oceans rise the vibrant cities that the majority of Wisconsinites call home. A freighter tugging impatiently at its anchor symbolizes Wisconsin's Great Lakes link with the wider world. On the other hand, whisking along on the I-highways, it's easy to ignore Wisconsin's small towns. But if you turn off and drive around the picture-postcard square or stop in at the local tavern, you can sense something of the nature of America's backbone. The earliest tombstones in the cemetery up on the hill read 1840 and 1850—Atwoods, Taylors, Joeckels, Fargos—strong-minded people who came a long way to be independent.

You can find Wisconsin in the inventive industry that is hers. The first successful automobile, the outboard motor, and the grain binder are among the important discoveries by Wisconsinites. But the typewriter may be the state's most significant invention. It revolutionized business practices, and women's proficiency in operating it did much to overcome the notion that a woman's place was in the home. Christopher Sholes, Carlos Glidden, and Samuel Soule developed the first typewriter in a building across the street from the present *Milwaukee Journal* offices. They patented the device in 1868 and sold the rights to Remington in 1873. Business and women have never been the same.

Also in Milwaukee, most of Wisconsin's famous beer is brewed. Surprisingly enough, it was three Welshmen who built the state's first brewery, in 1840. They were rapidly overtaken by a quartet of German brewers whose thirst-quenching names are with us still—Pabst, Blatz, Miller, and Schlitz.

It was not a fortune in furs, fish, or farmland that lured the first industrialists to Wisconsin; it was lead in the hills of the southwest. Some early miners came up from Illinois in the spring and retreated in the fall, like fish in a stream. They were called suckers. Others stuck it out year round, living in stone shelters that looked like dens. These miners were called badgers, and though their industry soon dwindled, their name left a lasting imprint on Wisconsin.

You can find Wisconsin in the classrooms, laboratories, and libraries of a great university. In February of 1849 Professor John Sterling rapped for order before a score of students in a borrowed classroom in the Madison Female Academy. Thus, without a building, a budget, or a president, the University of Wisconsin began. Over the years, the university has seen an agricultural chemist develop a cheap and rapid way to measure the butterfat content of milk; a historian speculate about the interplay of the frontier with the life, politics, and character of Americans; a ringing defense of academic freedom phrased; county agents trained to render the boundaries of the campus the boundaries of the state; a physics professor fabricate a pioneer educational radio station; generations of Wisconsin youths savor the moment between halves of a football game to sing the mighty "Varsity."

Today the University of Wisconsin is one of the ten largest and most distinguished universities in the country, serving some 38,000 students in Madison, 24,000 in Milwaukee, and 80,000 more at twenty-five other campuses throughout the state.

11

The Wind Point lighthouse, on Lake Michigan north of Racine—Stan Feiker

You can find Wisconsin in the spirit of the youths who marched out of the state's Camp Randalls to defend their country: the Black Hats of Wisconsin's Iron Brigade storming the approaches to Antietam and swinging down a Pennsylvania pike to a rendezvous with history at Gettysburg; lumberjacks turned engineers building a dam that saved a Union fleet; a governor's wife earning the affectionate nickname "the Wisconsin angel" as a hospital nurse in the forerunner of the Red Cross; the Red Arrow 32nd sacrificing itself in Belleau Wood; 332,000 Badgers serving in uniform around the globe in World War II.

You can find Wisconsin in all these things, for they are all Wisconsin. But you can most surely find the essence of the state in the beauty of her landscape. Every country window in Wisconsin is a charmed casement opening on rocks and rills, woods and templed hills, fruited plains and foaming seas. And it matters not a whit that these are not listed among the world's wonders.

The frontispiece of the scene from our cabin is a magnificent American elm, not yet struck down by beetles. Its circumference testifies that it was sown a century ago. In its marvelous pendulant branches is the swaying cradle of Baltimore orioles. At the base of our elm runs J. Jones Road. We can count on at least two vehicles to come past each day. One belongs to the mailman, who brings us the weekly, mimeographed Barneveld *News*. The postman's friendly wave is a signal that all is well along the Potomac. The other vehicle is the morning milk truck, going up to Ernie and Albert Peterson's place to pick up a bit of America's Dairyland that will find its way, perchance, to a cheese counter in Costa Mesa, California, where my granddaughter will pick it out. That we are on a mail-and-milk route means our road is plowed in winter, and there's nothing like a snowplow to double your pleasure in a Wisconsin winter.

Beyond J. Jones Road we can see the west end of a pond, sparkling under the massage of a brisk breeze. The wind has come from Missoula, Montana, across fecund fields of Iowa corn. From our window we cannot see the east end of the pond. Perhaps it runs on and on to nameless oceans. Across the pond the ground pitches sharply upward to form a rugged ridge. We cannot see the crest from our window. We know it to be 800 feet in elevation, but from our perspective it could be an 8,000-foot crag in Colorado. Birches mingle with oaks and hickories on the sharp slope. At their feet is a seasonal parade of wildflowers. In spring, a graceful doe may lead her fractious fawn down to the pond, and we can certainly count on a cock grouse to drum the announcement that he had prior claim to an acre or two, despite what our abstract of title may say.

The Sauk County village of Leland—
Ken Dequaine

But our corner of Wisconsin does not have a monopoly on beauty. There is, for example, a small northern lake to which I make an annual pilgrimage in August—over a railroad bridge, along a tamarack swamp, and through the hazel thickets. The painted turtles drop from the willow stumps in the slough along the tracks. A breeze displays the white sides of the maple leaves to give the woods a fresh and flowing look. As I near the lake, a flock of startled teal jumps out, and the sky is soon full of wheeling waterfowl. They circle the blue water swiftly, gracefully, now outlined dark against the sky, now flashing white against the tamaracks. When I hunker down in the cattails, they come to rest again, their soft conversation saying, "All clear."

But the "all clear" for scenery is not automatic. John Muir was a Wisconsin farm boy who educated himself at night after working sixteen hours in the fields. At the age of twenty-two he went to the University of Wisconsin, where he was recognized as a genius at mechanical inventions. But an accident temporarily handicapped him, and Muir became, by his own admission, "a tramp," exploring America's scenic wonders. Carefully recording what he saw, Muir gradually began to write and lecture, awakening his fellow citizens to the preservation of natural beauty. The Sierra Club he founded in 1892 played a crucial role in the creation of our system of national parks and wilderness areas. In Wisconsin, a dozen scenic areas bear his name.

In April of 1948 the sun glinted brightly on the swollen Wisconsin River. In the air was the piquant smell of grass-smoke as farmers went about their annual burning. Down in Sauk County, one fire got out of hand. A neighbor ran over to help. He filled a bucket with water and disappeared into the billowing smoke. He never came back. And yet the man never really left. He was Aldo Leopold, professor, father of wilderness areas, framer of Wisconsin's Conservation Commission, founder of the science of game management, and author of *A Sand County Almanac*, whose stirring essays have played a mighty role in inspiring America's present demand for environmental husbandry.

In 1952 a young Green Bay attorney took on the power companies and the Wisconsin Public Service

14

Lake Michigan and the harbor at Kenosha—Joseph Fire

Mallards taking flight in Ozaukee County—
Vern Arendt

Commission. He wanted to halt construction of a dam on the scenic Namekagon River, eighty miles of wilderness turbulence that snakes through Wisconsin's northwest woods. Virgil Muench pled has case before the state Supreme Court. In a landmark decision, the Court said: "The right of the citizens of the state to enjoy our navigable waters for recreational purposes, including the enjoyment of scenic beauty, is a legal right that is entitled to all the protection which is given financial rights."

It is fitting that this should be so. From the moment the Pilgrims dropped anchor in the shelter of Plymouth Rock, we have been children of open spaces. There was at hand the forest in all its primeval arrogance. Beyond were great prairies and mountains running to unknown oceans. It was a geography written on by few, a history unmade, an inland empire to shape and fill.

In Wisconsin, trappers penetrated the wilderness, lead miners followed them to make a frontier, lumberjacks cleared the forests, farmers poured in, railways hacked their way across the savanna. Little wonder that when we modern Wisconsinites look for meaning in life, we seek it in a forest, by a lake, or at the edge of a river. The out-of-doors is our inspiration, an opportunity to recapture, if only on a picnic in a park, a sense of that magic potion of wide skies and free minds that is our heritage.

Wisconsin is still an open land, full of space. It is still a country of striking beauty. Stand on a bank of the Mississippi, for example, and watch that green giant wind its way to Louisiana. Come upon a hidden lake in the bucolic hills of the Kettle Moraine. Drive along Main Street of a small town in all its charm. Travel into the shoulder country of northwestern Wisconsin's eroded mountains, each rise opening new vistas, until you can see the might of Lake Superior glistening in the sunset.

Clay Schoenfeld

Hepaticas in Columbia County—Charles Steinhacker, Nature Photography of America

16

Spring

Down along the north slope of the Ferry Bluff, Walter Moely's sugar bush came to life late every winter—an extensive grove of very old and very young soft maple trees growing away from the hill into the bottomland along Honey Creek where it wound through the woods to the Wisconsin. At its edge, where the road passed along the base of the hill, stood the syrup camp—a sturdy cabin backed with rows of wood collected and piled there during the summer and autumn months against the maple syrup season, which began with soft weather any time in February or March and lasted often as long as six or eight weeks, depending upon the vagaries of the weather and the stamina of Walter Moely, a lean, taciturn, laconic man, one of few words, who had for many years made maple syrup there and took pleasure in doing so, though his labors often stretched far into the night and, once the sap was cooking, kept him constantly alert getting in wood, firing, settling the boiling sap, testing and drawing off the syrup.

There was something about this solitary occupation that drew me to the sugar bush, particularly at night—perhaps for its reflection of time past, for nothing here had changed very much save perhaps in the bush, where around some of the great old maples tubing had replaced some of the spiles. But the pails still hung from the trees, hundreds of them, glinting in the moonlight, and, walking among the trees, I would hear the sap dripping from the spiles as the sound of bells far beyond the horizon; and the sap cooked and bubbled and frothed in the shallow pans, filling the cabin with fragrance, and sending great gouts of steam through the vents in the roof; and the fire glowed whenever Walter opened the stove and put in more wood; and the sparks flew upward among the budded trees to be lost among the stars. Here, deep in the woods, isolated among the ancient boles, life burgeoned every winter, sometimes with snow still deep on the ground. Far to the north passed the highway, and the lights of farms shone across the meadows between the sugar bush and the highway, but here in this solitary place one man's industry turned all the hidden sweetness of the maples into fragrant steam and delicately flavored syrup and succulent sugar. . . .

What drew me there, night after night in the season was the solitude, the tangibility of spring in the sap surging upward to drop from the spiles into the buckets, making a little night music there, the tenuous continuity with time past, and even, at leave-taking, the sparks riding into heaven. I used to watch, standing outside the cabin, how the sparks rode the draft from the chimney, charging aloft among the maple branches hanging over, driving toward the amber eye of Arcturus shining there on many evenings, brief stars rising through the smoke and steam, red and yellow, only to wink out against the dark, while owls and foxes were abroad in equal wonder at what went on here so far from the haunts of men.

August Derleth

Walter Moely's sugar bush, near Sauk City—
Ken Dequaine

We are, each of us, like so many tin whistles, tuned to the range of notes that the country gives in definition of spring. That set of signals, when put together, triggers us to pack away long underwear, snow tires, and overshoes, and releases us to short-sleeved shirts and window screens.

Many define spring when the frogs start their chorus of *groaks* and *peeps* in the evening from damp hollows. Some get spring's start in the blooming of skunk cabbage or arbutus, or in the adventurous lavender blossoms of hepatica. Others find it in the appearance of all those tiny gray kittens that crawl out on the ends of willow branches. For others, it arrives when lacy red flowers are cast out by maple trees for coy lovemaking with the wind. A friend captured spring when he wrote a one-word letter. The word was *konkaree,* the untranslated adjective the redwing blackbird uses to describe its pleasure at seeing the creeks and rivers let loose from the hands of winter.

Farmers are tuned to a set of spring signals that tells them when it is time to begin plowing. The precise signals vary from farmer to farmer, for it is an internal clock that takes into consideration the amount of acreage to plow, the crops, and the clues the land gives that it is ready. Farmers who follow the advice of skunk cabbage are an ambitious sort, for the blooming plants are often covered by a March or April blizzard. Dandelions and watercress seem to be more reliable in their predictions, needing a thicker sense of sun-given comfort before they commence their green ambitions. Whatever sets it ticking, the plowing clock of farmers has been set and adjusted to an accuracy by generations; it has gained its reliability by experience.

Plowing is a primitive art, a country square-dance in which the farmer swings his earthy partner. There is pleasure in being at the beginning of the chain, where it all starts, all the politics, all the religion, all the industry. The plowman is at the head of the parade, at the place from which all nations draw their power. The land before the tractor seems plain—the tillage of glaciers, the grindings from eons of wind and rain, common muck and clay, Plainfield sand and Buena Vista loam—but it is an awesome sight, the humble temple of life and civilization.

Plowing is a symbolic task. Beyond its inherent usefulness lies a deeper meaning. Plowing illustrates the basic relationship between the field and the man. The bare brown earth is the only real resource; all others pale in comparison. No gold mine, oil well, or copper pit has any value at all if there is not somewhere an abundance of fertile brown fields.

Fresh-plowed ground has a subtle fragrance. The dead of millions of years are in the earth, all the beasts and flying things, all the grasses, trees, and bushes. But the soil is not so somber as to be a grave alone. If there are in it the bits and pieces of former lives, there are also the Tinkertoy parts for yet other lives, a gift the land just keeps passing around. Plowed ground

21

A male pine grosbeak—Brian Milne

The Eau Claire River at Eau Claire Dells County Park, in Marathon County—Tom Algire

smells of earthworms and empires.

The tractor seat is a good vantage point from which to watch the increasing lean toward spring. Plowing doesn't require much attention. The front right wheel of the tractor is dropped into the previously cut furrow, and the machine pretty much steers itself, needing only a light hand to steady the wheel. There is time to watch the prowling flight of hawks, riding in easy circles over the warming fields. Plowed ground has an attraction for horned larks, killdeer, redwing blackbirds, and white-eyed Brewer's blackbirds. They flit about on their missions of opportunity over the just-turned pages of the earth. Great blue herons take diagonal flight across the fields, making course for the river shallows and a vertebrate lunch. Squirrels adorn the trees, and if the tractor stops for a while, the squeaking of butternut-sized young can be heard from the dens. Flocks of geese fly overhead, working faint furrows into their own vast blue prairie fields. Their passage is a natural blessing, and the spring seems more promising if their flight passes over the new-plowed ground.

In the distance, the trees appear as lazy puffs of pale smoke from the green fire being rekindled there. But before the greening gets wildly contagious, the land is particularly naked, and there is a delight in seeing the hills and wide fields while they are immodestly dressed. It is a pleasure then to be a husbandman to the beauty that is the land.

Sometimes in the spring you can see a farmer walking his fields, getting on his knees to look closer at the ground. He puts his hand to the fresh-plowed earth, to feel it as a mother would feel the head of a child, checking for fevers or chills. The man holds the soil in his hand to let the moisture and fertility register in an

Fertile furrows near Mount Horeb, in Dane
County—Ken Dequaine

View from Mill Bluff State Park, in Monroe
County—Ken Dequaine

Near Independence, in Trempealeau County—
Ken Dequaine

invisible computer that gives the odds of success. When the farmer gets up and goes back to his tractor, his knees are soiled—the badge of his high ageless office. "Tillers of the Soil," said farmer Thomas Jefferson, "are the Chosen of the Lord."

And it must've been a farmer who wrote the words to the old Shaker hymn:

> 'Tis the gift to be simple,
> 'Tis the gift to be free,
> 'Tis the gift to come down
> Where we ought to be.
> And when we find ourselves
> In the place just right
> 'Twill be in the valley
> Of love and delight.

You can hear that hymn all across Wisconsin now. The land itself hums the tune from new-plowed ground. The melody can be heard above the noise of a diesel tractor throttled against the stop. It is a music made for spring plowing.

Justin Isherwood

A bloodroot along the Ice Age Trail in the Blue Hills region of Rusk County—Allen F. Hillery

There is much confusion between land and country. Land is the place where corn, gullies, and mortgages grow. Country is the personality of land, the collective harmony of its soil, life, and weather. Country knows no mortgages, no alphabetical agencies, no tobacco road; it is calmly aloof to these petty exigencies of its alleged owners. That the previous occupant of my farm was a bootlegger mattered not one whit to its grouse; they sailed as proudly over the thickets as if they were guests of a king.

Poor land may be rich country, and vice versa. Only economists mistake physical opulence for riches. Country may be rich despite a conspicuous poverty of physical endowment, and its quality may not be apparent at first glance, nor at all times.

I know, for example, a certain lakeshore, a cool austerity of pines and wave-washed sands. All day you see it only as something for the surf to pound, a dark ribbon that stretches farther than you can paddle, a monotony to mark the miles by. But toward sunset some vagrant breeze may waft a gull across a headland, behind which a sudden roistering of loons reveals the presence of a hidden bay. You are seized with an impulse to land, to set foot on bearberry carpets, to pluck a balsam bed, to pilfer beach plums or blueberries, or perhaps to poach a partridge from out those bosky quietudes that lie behind the dunes. A bay? Why not also a trout stream?

Incisively the paddles clip little
soughing swirls athwart the gunwale,
the bow swings sharp shoreward and
cleaves the greening depths for camp.

Later, a supper-smoke hangs lazily
upon the bay; a fire flickers under
drooping boughs. It is a lean poor land,
but rich country.

Some woods, perennially lush, are
notably lacking in charm. Tall
clean-boled oaks and tulip poplars may
be good to look at, from the road, but
once inside one may find a coarseness

A Green Bay shoreline north of Sturgeon
Bay—Sheldon Green

of minor vegetation, a turbidity of waters, and a paucity of wildlife. I cannot explain why a red rivulet is not a brook. Neither can I, by logical deduction, prove that a thicket without the potential roar of a quail covey is only a thorny place. Yet every outdoorsman knows that this is true. That wildlife is merely something to shoot at or to look at is the grossest of fallacies. It often represents the difference between rich country and mere land.

There are woods that are plain to look at, but not to look into. Nothing is plainer than a cornbelt woodlot; yet, if it be August, a crushed pennyroyal, or an over-ripe mayapple, tells you here is a place. October sun on a hickory nut is irrefutable evidence of good country; one senses not only hickory but a whole chain of further sequences: perhaps of oak coals in the dusk, a young squirrel browning, and a distant barred owl hilarious over his own joke.

The taste for country displays the same diversity in aesthetic competence among individuals as the taste for opera, or oils. There are those who are willing to be herded in droves through 'scenic' places; who find mountains grand if they be proper mountains, with waterfalls, cliffs, and lakes. To such the Kansas plains are tedious. They see the endless corn, but not the heave and the grunt of ox teams breaking the prairie. History, for them, grows on campuses. They look at the low horizon, but they cannot see it, as de Vaca did, under the bellies of the buffalo.

In country, as in people, a plain exterior often conceals hidden riches, to perceive which requires much living in and with. Nothing is more monotonous than the juniper foothills, until some veteran of a thousand summers, laden blue with berries, explodes in a blue burst of chattering jays. The drab sogginess of a March cornfield, saluted by one honker from the sky, is drab no more.

Aldo Leopold

Early spring in a Marathon County cornfield—
Tom Algire

Where the Peshtigo River bends down and around layers of bedrock that cut across the earth like ribs, there is a place called Roaring Rapids. If you go to that place you can see how the river rolls timelessly across the slanting shelf, beating the rock smooth, washing it into sand, a bit here, a bit there. And if you are quiet, you can hear strange things happening inside the river.

Down there in the water, stones are moving—big ones and small ones bumping downstream. The Peshtigo is rolling stones, flowing stones, a stone river washing away at its bedrock with water and brute boulders.

Over the centuries, the river has probably rolled thousands of rocks hundreds of miles. In the early days, after the glaciers, the Peshtigo must have been a swollen tide of stone. We cannot penetrate the past to see that secret time, but we know that there was rare cataclysm, violent upheaval, long, long years of grinding. Now each stone comes down from an upstream place as a river within a river, moving perhaps an inch a month, fetching up against unyielding rock, working its way along over years beyond counting.

We cannot know what is really happening down there under the burnished flow, where the water streams like cold silk across the ancient bed of mountains. Like a cosmic clock ticking fitfully, we hear the stones thud dully, marking time in no manner we can ever hope to record. The stone river foams sand and pebbles, waves hulking boulders. It swells under our lives with the low rumble of rolling mountains, restless seas, lowering skies raining down for centuries—eternal thunder sounding deep in the water where no lightning strikes.

Larry Van Goethem

The South Fork of the Flambeau River—
Tom Algire

There it was, the low, unmistakable rumble of white water. We nosed the canoe around a point thickly cloaked with white cedar and straightened the boat to the quickening current. Before us lay the historic St. Croix River, walled in by dense stands of second-growth evergreens. And dead ahead were the white horses of Scout Chute—bucking and kicking. As the banks closed in, the river accelerated. We could feel it, under us and around us, strong and unrelenting, sweeping us inexorably into the notch of the first dark V. The bow heaved upward, slamming a standing wave and bursting it into droplets suspended in crystalline blue-whiteness. An eternity of moments later, we shot onto the flat water below.

Far in the geologic past, two giant fault zones extended south from Lake Superior into this broad valley. They guided glaciers into the basin, and the ice carved a route to what one day, when men got around to naming things, would be known as the Mississippi River. When the enormous masses of ice dwindled before the warm sun of a new age, Lake Superior brimmed and sent a part of its overflow cascading through the valley. Gradually, however, as the earth's crust was relieved of the crushing burden of ice, the land slowly rose, separating the St. Croix from the inland sea. The rising land mass created two famous rivers. The fabled Brule rises within half a mile of the springs that are the source of the St. Croix. One flows northward,

Ducknest Rapids, on the Wolf River in
Menominee County—Tom Algire

ultimately to add its clear, cold waters to those of the great lake; the other streams away to union with the Mississippi.

There has been change, of course. First came the great forests, which healed the wounds wrought by glacial bulldozing. Much later, beginning late in the 1600s, came the voyageurs and trappers, who moved like shadows, leaving hardly more than the spent coals of their campfires to tell of their passing. After them came the men who wrested untold fortunes in pine lumber from the St. Croix and its tributaries. The virgin forests are gone now, yet the river itself remains much as it has always been. So, on a flawless spring day, we came to the St. Croix, lured by a sense of its history and by the bright promise of fishing and exploring. There is, after all, a magical quality to a river float; it combines the idyll of Huck Finn rafting with the precarious existence of a riverboat gambler.

We moved down the swift river as if on a long, descending staircase. Every now and then we startled a wood duck or a merganser. And once, a small doe, up to her brisket in cool water, regarded our boats as they slid quietly past. As the day flowed away in a succession of rapids, the canoe sped silently through midafternoon shadows to the sound of rushing water and warblers calling surreptitiously from streamside. The sun slanted into our eyes and turned the river to dancing stabs of gold and yellow.

The Mississippi River at Perrot State Park—
Ken Dequaine

In the fading light of a golden evening, we watched a flock of cedar waxwings launch themselves from the top of a white pine into an invisible swarm of insects. By the embers of the campfire, we talked about the river and its past. How, in the late 1600s, Daniel Greysolon de Dulhut ascended the frigid and trout-rich waters of the Brule from Lake Superior. How, with help from a Chippewa guide, he found the two-mile portage that leads from the headwaters of the Brule to the source of the St. Croix. Dulut thought he had found the Northwest Passage, that elusive portal to the riches of the East. He had found instead a water route from the greatest of the Great Lakes to the Mississippi basin. And for a nation dependent upon the glossy pelt of the beaver for much of its national wealth, that was quite enough.

Roger Drayna

A white-tailed deer in a poplar grove at Rock Island State Park—George R. Cassidy

Flowers and mushrooms on a sphagnum floor near Ashland—Robert McQuilkin

A northern forest—Charles F. Davis

The surface of the St. Croix River—Tom Algire

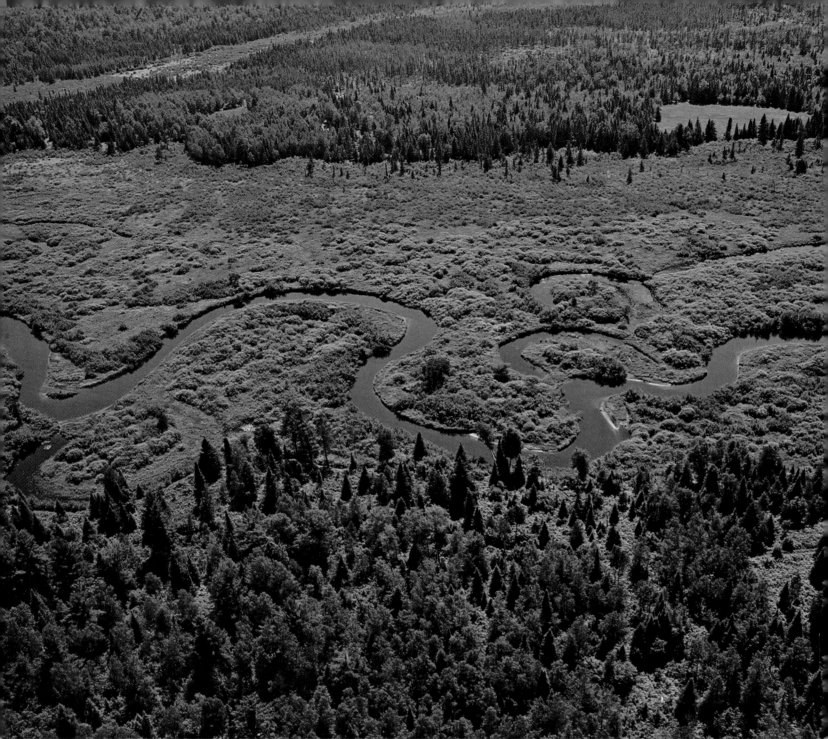

Meanders and oxbows on an Oneida County
stream—Vern Arendt

We slip so easily into spring. All it takes, it seems, is a sunny day, a gentle breeze, and all of the memories of a cold and bitter winter vanish as quickly as a dry fly in an alder tangle. Sometimes a telephone call helps speed things along. Del Richardson called early last week and said, "We're planning a little fishing trip Wednesday. How about I pick you up about seven?" And that's the way it begins, nice and easy. There is just the phone call, announcing quietly that the clan is gathering once again. A few plans are made, and the first fishing trip of the year is on.

I remember once coming off a stream and walking toward a bridge where Bud Laugen was leaning on a railing, waiting for me. I was wearing the traditional battered hat, vest, and waders. A wooden-handled net hung by my side. I carried a fine Fenwick fly rod. My creel was empty. Laugen waited until I got within earshot. Then I heard him say, "I don't understand it. You *look* like a trout fisherman."

Laugen is inclined to fish with night crawlers, but he doesn't always, and even when he doesn't, he is more than likely to turn up with the biggest trout. And I don't understand that, because he doesn't look at all like a trout fisherman. He wears an old pair of brush pants, the same ones he wears for grouse hunting, deer hunting, and muskie fishing, and I wouldn't be at all surprised if he slept in them. Before he puts his hip boots on, he carefully removes and stores in the trunk of the car an old pair of Romeo slippers, the kind with elastic sides that old men are so fond of. He pulls on a gaudy, bright green jacket and covers that with a ratty looking trout vest with worm stains all over it.

Then he rigs up a battered old fly rod, of which he is exceedingly fond and protective. It is not a Fenwick. I once picked it up to see what kind it was, but he yanked it away from me before I could get a good look at it.

If there is a little chill in the air, he covers his head with a down hood that ties in a neat little bow under his chin. Then he stuffs a chew of Plow Boy in the corner of his mouth, and if it weren't for the fact that he was cackling and giggling like an old woman, you'd swear you were watching a giant bunny rabbit hopping off toward the stream.

But there's no mistaking it—he is a first-rate trout fisherman, and I'd gladly turn in my Fenwick, and even throw in the waders and net, for just a little of what he knows about trout fishing.

Last week three of us split up on a Richland County stream, with plans to meet again in time for lunch. Del and I headed a few miles upstream from the other two. Del put in by a small bridge along a gravel road. I drove up to where the stream narrows and runs between high banks through a tangle of trees and brush. I got out and looked at the stream. It bubbled and gurgled over its rocky bed. Birds sang from the trees. I could hear a ruffed grouse drumming in a thicket behind me.

This is the part I wait for, when I am alone by a trout stream. I begin doing all the familiar things, slowly and methodically, and I can feel the slowing down, the draining away of the tensions. I uncoil last year's leader and run it through a piece of old rubber inner tube to take out the kinks. I carefully and patiently tie a new tippet on the end.

Del has provided me with an assortment of his favorite flies. Killers, he calls them. They are the black bomber, the muskrat's regret, and the squirrel tail, all freshly tied and brand spanking new. I tie on a black bomber and head down the bank and toward the stream. A redwing blackbird scolds as I pass. It is good to be walking again on bare ground, to feel the grass

43

beneath my waders, to feel the familiar rush of cold water when I step into the stream.

The first few casts are disastrous. It's been a long fall and winter, and I am on my third black bomber before I finally am in control of my rod and line. It is warm, and soon I have removed my sweater and tied it around my waist. In shirt-sleeves, I climb up on the bank and light my pipe and sit in the sun, enjoying the warmth on my face and bare arms.

Back in the stream, I move slowly, enjoying the rhythm of fly casting, the soft whistle of the line working above my head. There is one strike, which I miss. It bothers me not at all. There will be plenty of time for the catching of fish, and even I will catch a few. The law of averages decrees it. This day is a celebration of spring, of running water, of sunshine, of all the good days that now are only beginning.

Three hours pass quickly. Del has fished up to the car, and now I hear him out on the road. I climb the bank and wave. We drive downstream and hunt for Laugen. Eventually we spot him picking his way through a thicket at the edge of the stream. He is oblivious to our presence until our honking and shouting finally get his attention. Laugen is not young, but he walks to the car with the spring of youth in his step. He is smiling. He has removed his bunny hood. When he crosses the fence, he makes a great show of protecting the canvas creel that hangs from his shoulder. "Kept three," he says, opening the creel to display three glistening brown-trout, the largest about eleven inches.

"I just don't understand it," I tell him. "You don't look like a trout fisherman at all."

Steve Hopkins

44

Near Sarona, in Washburn County—
John Cushman

Iowa County, part of the Driftless Area—
William E. Ruth

Norseville School, near Foster, in Eau Claire
County—Ken Dequaine

"Everything is turning into plastic," Bill Leinenkugel told me. "The other day my wife gave me a cup of coffee, and it was made out of solubles or something. She put in another thing called Sprinkle, a chemical sugar, and then I added something called Pream, plastic, I think. I took a look in the cup and realized there wasn't anything real in the whole business."

Bill Leinenkugel is something of an endangered species these days. At Chippewa Falls, he runs a small family-owned brewery in an era that has seen the small brewery go the way of the trolley car and the straw boater. He survives by making sure there's nothing the least bit plastic about his beer. The Leinenkugels have been brewing beer in Wisconsin ever since 1845, when Matthias, the patriarch and master brewer, arrived from Prussia.

We were barreling along the shore of Lake Wissota in Bill Leinenkugel's old Ford while we tracked down one of his drivers. "There's one of our competitors," he said. I looked around. No building in sight. A few men in sport shirts and loose slacks—a long way off—were ambling across the meadow. Beyond them, a white truck, unmarked, lumbered through the grass.

"The white truck there," I said. "That's Walter's Brewing from Eau Claire, right?"

"Right," Bill Leinenkugel answered. "I wish we had a couple more like Walter. Small breweries make for good competition—the kind that results in *better* beer, not just more of it."

I had swum in the amber Chippewa at first light that morning, before driving into town along the west bank of the river. Highway 178 twists in such a maddening way that it seems to have been laid down by a pastry chef. But to drive it slowly and watch the debut of a spring day—crows calling, cows bent to shadowed fields, early bees hovering in the blue spiderwort along the bank—is to be seized hard yet one more time by the immeasurable beauty that is Wisconsin. The Chippewa grows broader as it nears Lake Wissota, lies absolutely still, and when I stopped the car at its strangeness and walked over to its edge, I saw the river had become sky: pale blue, first clouds floating, trees on the far bank growing straight down dark and green into the perfect image.

As I came into downtown Chippewa Falls, I passed an old-timer in a neat gray suit with a white handkerchief tucked in his breast pocket sitting in a chair in the long low sunlight out front of the Hotel Northern. He was reading the sports section of the morning paper, and from his air of weary desperation, I identified him at once as a Cubs fan. I found a diner and had breakfast before starting out for Leinenkugel's. The brewery is toward the north edge of town. It is an agglomeration tied together with red brick and mortar over the years—part old, part new, and all as neat and tidy as an elderly nun. Painted high on the side of the latest section, alongside the Leinenkugel Indian maiden with her demure red mouth and a red-tipped feather stuck in her red headband, are the words: "Home of Leinenkugel's Beer. Famous Since 1867. Made with Spring Water." (Everything in Chippewa Falls is made with spring water. They sell it around the country in bottles and take baths in it at home. If you try to bring regular common ordinary water into Chippewa Falls, they arrest you. It's a crime classed with offering oleo to a dairy farmer.)

Leinenkugel's has been brewed on this site for more than a century. Imagine the malt in its hopper, high in the brewhouse, the room hot and close, the hot-water tanks nearby pulsing like huge gray beasts. Then descend from the light cereal smell of this floor to the level of the mash tun, where the grainy fragrance is so rich and heavy it makes the air edible. Here, the malt and corn and spring water are heated and rotated in the big tun until they become wort. This pale amber liquid is strained into the lauter tub and thence to the massive copper brew-kettle sunk in the red stone floor. Here, the wort will be brewed with hops for its proper sharp tang.

From the brew kettle, descend even further to where the hops are strained away. Then climb back up three stories through cooling coils to the stout white tanks of the fermenting cellar. Here, the brew is pitched with yeast and fermentation begins. For almost two weeks, the beer lies in a chilly room that hums like a submarine. Then it is pumped to the aging cellar, where the atmosphere is even stronger and sharper than beer. In this room, so cold the tangle of pipes is enveloped in heavy white frost, the brew rests more than a month. Then it is led out once again, this time down into the tanks of the finishing cellar, where it is filtered, carbonated, completed. After ten days in this cellar, we have Leinenkugel's Beer.

It struck me that I was watching serious men at a serious business, and I went and asked Bill Leinenkugel about it. "Brewery workers *are* different, truthfully," he said. "My grandmother told me that you always should pay your men well because when they get off work, others will expect them to buy a round occasionally. So when the men in the woods were making a dollar a day, the men at the brewery were making a dollar and a half. But they were also the brewery's ambassadors of good will. The average small-brewery worker is more loyal than any other worker in American industry." Bill Leinenkugel didn't sound like a man at bay, yet the statistics on survival of small breweries are ominous, and he knows it. There are only a handful left in the country.

On my way home, I stopped for a

Copper brew-kettles at the Pabst Brewing Company, in Milwaukee—George Gambsky

cold bottle of Leinenkugel's at the bar in the hotel. It was fine beer, big and hearty and lively. The old-timer was still in the green metal chair out in front. The sun was coming around and would soon be working on his cold side. He had the new issue of *Time* in his hands and was paging through it with the look of a man at a smorgasbord. I thought: "These are people who endure."

Driving back up the river, I hoped that Bill Leinenkugel and the workers he considers part of the family would endure, too. If we lose their kind of small business, their kind of attitude toward work and quality, we will have taken another giant step into the age of plastic. If Leinenkugel goes, it won't be merely the brewing industry that has been diminished. It will be all of us.

Michael O'Malley

Morning mist over a north-country lake—
Richard H. Smith, Earth Imagery

But I, when I undress me
Each night, upon my knees
Will ask the Lord to bless me
With apple pie and cheese.

Those pious lines are Eugene Field's, but their piety did not originate with him. "Many's the night I dreamed of cheese—toasted, mostly," said Ben Gunn, recalling his years as a castaway on Treasure Island. One of Shakespeare's trenchermen hurried a dinner because "There's pippins and cheese to come!" And Field's own verses may have been inspired by the ancient English rhyme: "An apple-pie without some cheese/Is like a kiss without a squeeze."

Cheese making probably dates almost from the time men first stole milk from animals. "Cheese of the kine" was given to David more than three thousand years ago, and there are other references to it in the Old Testament. In the absence of contrary evidence, it is permissible to theorize that cheese was invented by accident and—like truffles, caviar, shellfish, rattlesnakes, ants, and other gourmet delicacies—first eaten by somebody who was either very hungry, very courageous, or very parsimonious. Primitive cheeses could have been no more than sour milk curds drained of their whey. With the possible exception of Miss Muffet, nobody would have preferred them to milk or cream or butter. But unlike the fresh dairy products, even the early cheeses could be stored for long periods and carried on long journeys—a vital advantage, especially in biblical climates.

From its humble and purely utilitarian origins, cheese has become one of the richest and most varied of the table graces, no more to be defined as a food than wine is to be defined as a drink. Cheese makers, like vintners, have made their science what every science ought to be: a handmaiden in the service of art. Indeed, fermented spirits are the only product native to as many cultures as cheese. Both are made by all the civilized and most of the uncivilized peoples. When I travel to a strange land, the first thing I do is sample its liquor and its cheese, usually together, because they usually *go* together. Cheese has a natural affinity to spirits. Now that I think of it, cheese has a natural affinity to just about everything.

Sybarites who take a special pleasure in cheese, and a special delight in exploring its infinite varieties, are known to *Webster's Unabridged* as turophiles. The true turophile is a peaceable chap, gentle and reflective in most matters, but not to be stopped by a charge of bears when he scents a new cheese, be it an *–ost* from Norway or a *–bo* from Denmark or a yaks'-milk cheese from a lamasery in Tibet. North of Oslo, I was served reindeer-milk cheese from Lapland. Ugh? Well, yes. But if I can ever get to India, there's a cheese made from water-buffalo milk . . .

It's at least arguable that Wisconsin satisfies turophilia better than any other enclave on our little globe. France produces more *kinds* of cheese than Wisconsin, but few of the 400-odd French cheeses can be found very far from the communes, villages, or individual farms where they are made. Any one of the cheese depots along our highways offers the traveler a broader spectrum from which to choose than can be easily found in all of Paris. In Switzerland the range is even shorter. It's harder to buy feta or Havarti in Switzerland than it used to be to buy margarine—I write that word with an effort—in Wisconsin. Britain, Holland, Germany, Belgium (whence sprang Limburger), and Scandinavia all make splendid cheeses, but no longer innovate or even imitate. Their turophiles, unless they can afford either to travel or to pay stiff import duties, must satiate their passion on *fromages du pays*.

Few of the world's great cheeses are of Yankee origin. Liederkranz is an American cheese, and so is Monterey Jack. As a native New Englander, I am embarrassed to report that Vermont's once-great sage cheese is now made with imitation sage leaves. But because God meant sage cheese to be consumed with mashed-potato doughnuts, which have also vanished, the loss of genuine sage cheese only nails down an already half-shut window on Paradise.

One of Wisconsin's noble contributions to the art is Colby cheese, but there's a mystery about this. Colby, Wisconsin, greets you with a sign proclaiming it to be the home of Colby cheese. A historical marker attributes it to a Joseph Steinwand, who discovered his new cheese in 1885 and named it for the Town in which his father, Ambrose, had built northern Clark County's first cheese factory, three years before. The mystery is that these facts have apparently eluded the lexicographers. The *Encyclopaedia Britannica* doesn't include Colby in its list of major cheeses, perhaps under the misapprehension that it's a trade name. *Webster's* says, confusedly, that Colby is "prob. from the name Colby," a lexicologist's way of saying "I dunno." The *Encyclopedia of Cheeses* distributed by the World of Cheese Club describes Colby as a type of Cheddar used mostly for manufacturing purposes and imported from "other countries such as Australia, New Zealand, etc." (Steady, Colby Chamber of Commerce! I am corresponding with these pundits.)

Although an extreme case, Colby is not the only community whose cheese has eloped with its identity. Gorgonzola, Wensleydale, Emmenthal, Cheddar, Glarus, Stilton, Limburger, Gruyère, and other place-names mean cheeses to millions of people for every one to whom they mean places.

Wisconsin earned, and holds, its high place on the cheese board less as inventor than as emulator. It produces most of the Old World cheeses, many so good as to be indistinguishable from the best imports. Not all, however. Wisconsin Swiss cannot quite equal Swiss Swiss; our blue cheeses must yield the courtesy of the road to Denmark's Danablu; and nobody makes Roquefort like a Frenchman—or should I say like a French ewe? Cows' milk is used here. (These are personal opinions. Different taste-buds tell different stories. In quiet, cultivated discussions with other turophiles, my preferences have got my coffee spilled and my shirt torn.) But our Edams and Goudas are as good as any from the Netherlands, and Somerset Maugham, who lived most of his life in France, considered Wisconsin Camembert as good as French.

But our greatest cheese glory is our Cheddar. There are others, true: Vermont's glistening white Cheddar, Canada's lovely golden Cheddar, the tangy Cheddars from New York's Herkimer County, and, of course, the original Cheddar from Cheddar, where it has been made for four centuries. These are all superb cheeses. But none approaches Wisconsin's Cheddar in its rainbow of variations and harmonic subtleties—flavored with bacon or cured with smoke, sprinkled

with caraway or sesame seeds, cubed or coned or wheeled or potted as a spread, mild as a sister's kiss or sharp enough to bring tears (of joy) to your eyes. And if the shop you're in doesn't have exactly the Cheddar you dreamed about last night, there's a place just down the highway that will.

A place like Lemke's, for example. Partly for help with this essay, partly drawn by a most heavenly aroma, I visited Wausau's Lemke Cheese Company. Not one of the giants, Lemke's is believed to be the only Wisconsin plant to produce, cure, and package five different cheeses under one roof: brick, Mozzarella, Colby, Cheddar, and Muenster. Owner-manager Bud Lemke was too busy to see me, too nice not to, and too justifiably proud of his cheese making to lose a chance to talk about it. He explained that the firm had been founded by his father in 1929 and that its lifetime goal had been not just excellence but *consistency* of excellence in its products. Its success has attracted commercial customers from all across the country. I saw racks with thousands of labels, all carrying the Lemke name and the words "Packed for," followed by the names of various private vendors and distributors who have come to rely on Lemke quality. When I incautiously doubted that anybody could invest brick cheese with real character, Bud gave me a specimen of Lemke brick. Believe me, it has character.

Dairy interests have sometimes used questionable promotion to exploit cheese, which is too bad, because if ever there was a product supremely able to promote itself, it's cheese. Unwilling to depend on piety or patriotism, Wisconsin's legislators once enacted a law forbidding restaurants to serve pie unaccompanied by cheese. Our solons prudently provided no penalty for noncompliance, but if anything could make me eat pie minus cheese (nothing could), it would be a law like that.

Another mistake in the cheese literature is its studied avoidance of words like *smelly* or *moldy*. The smelly cheeses are decorously described as "full-bodied" or "robust"; moldy cheese is "blue-veined" or "piquant." I suspect this nice-Nellyism costs the cheese industry more customers than it gains. Many great cheeses *are* smelly or moldy. The beginner beckoned to

Limburger, Backstein, or Romadur by an understatement like "robust" may not be able to get the cheese past his nose and is unlikely to try again.

Urging people to eat cheese for health purposes is still another ploy of questionable effect. No doubt cheese is good for us, and so is spinach, but no food, sport, art, diversion, or human practice appeals to people on the ground that it's good for them. The committed turophile loves cheese in *spite* of the fact that it's good for him.

Cheese country is to be explored, not carried by assault. The cheese adventure is a leisurely ramble in pleasant places, amid temptations it is the explorer's Christian duty not to resist but to yield to. But he should keep moving. His palate, pampered by old favorites, should also be continuously stimulated by new challenges.

If you are not ready for Limburger, don't jump to it; sneak up on it by way of sharp Cheddar, French Muenster, Bel Paese, and Liederkranz. After these, you'll find Limburger a superb accompaniment to pumpernickel bread. The road to Stilton—England's "King of Cheeses," served in all baronial halls with brandy and cigars after the ladies have retired—lies through blue cheese, Camembert, Roquefort, and the Gorgonzolas. The miracle of these and other journeys in cheese country is that the turophile does not leave his multiplying discoveries behind him. He carries them with him along a road with no end.

"Have you tried this one, sir?" inquires the young lady lucky enough to work behind a cheese counter. (I often wonder what the cheese clerk buys one-half so precious as the stuff she sells.) She deftly peels off a sliver and offers it to me with a cracker. No, I hadn't tried it; and certainly, I'll take a quarter of a pound. And if Eleanor reminds me of the capacity of the icebox and wants to know where I'm going to put it, I know where I'm going to put it.

I know plenty of people who'll help me put it there, too.

Digby B. Whitman

On Lake Wingra, in Madison—Don Davenport

Summer

I am always going back to see if the big, black clams still cluster along the clay bottoms of the winding Rock River, hoping to find one with a pearl luminous as the moon. It is an unfinished piece of business that has been smoldering like gold fever since the day, as a sun-dried crisp of a boy, my questing thumb felt through a mess of clam meat and juice, touched the first hard nubbin of pearl, and turned it to the light, where it flashed pale pink and white and light blue in the blazing sun. I held the seed pearl in the palm of my callused hand, and my fingers trembled so much the pearl quivered with opalescent light. Then and there, any plans my mother had for making me into a concert violinist drained like rain off a hill to become one with my mysterious river.

The idea that my beautiful and bountiful river could hold such riches as might tempt grown men came late in life. I was already ten, and though I knew where the terns and coots nested, what sloughs to spear carp in, what bays held the largest northerns, which gravel bars the walleyes came to after dark, I had never dreamed that somewhere along that coppery river might rest a clam with a pearl big as a pigeon's egg and brilliant as the flame of the candle that each night lighted the way to my cot on the porch.

In the beginning, I knew nothing of pearls, nothing of the men who hunted them. Then one night, having gone to my cot, I lay listening for the splash of fish on the river, the inquiry of a night heron, the whimper of the little owls in the oaks. Then came a strange sound, and lifting to an elbow so I could look through the screen, I saw flashlight beams crisscrossing the glade. Next morning there was a tent, and I discovered that one woman and two men had moved in during the night, though for what—for they had no fish poles—I couldn't imagine. When they

began bringing boatloads of big, black clams to shore, when they sat cross-legged opening them, discarding the shell and flesh, I was mystified. But having, like a young brush buck, an aversion to coming too close to strangers, I stayed my distance and waited until that night to ask my father what they might be doing.

"Likely looking for pearls," he said.

Pearls! In my Rock River! I didn't sleep much that night. The next morning I threaded my duck skiff along their trail, careful to stay a respectable distance. When they began collecting clams, I put out some cane poles—with no bait on the hooks—so they wouldn't know I was spying. Without removing any of their clothes, the men waded chest deep in the river, feeling for the clams with their feet and dunking at intervals to bring them up.

I wrapped and stowed my poles and hastened around a bend so I'd be out of sight. Then I began collecting clams. When I had a black mound of them in the stern of the little skiff, I paddled back to the cottage, got a knife, and sat down to open them. But the harder I tried, the tighter the clams closed their shells. I tried smashing them between two rocks. They broke open, but the flesh was crushed, and juice spattered on my bare legs. I scraped and bruised and cut my fingers, but I found no pearls.

I remember as though it were yesterday when I finished with the last clam. The sun was boiling down out of a brassy sky. A cloud of flies had descended on the clams and me. My fingers were crisscrossed with cuts. The clam juice was congealing on my body in uncomfortable and alien scabs. In the end, it was the flies rather than an overwhelming desire to find pearls that drove me back into the river to get another load of clams.

I went through the whole painful procedure again but found no pearls. I

Weird weir—Mary Brzezinski

Formations named Sugar Bowl and Grotto Rock,
in the lower Wisconsin Dells—Ken Dequaine

think that might have ended it, but the next day, when I walked into Juneau to deliver bullheads to the Northwestern Hotel, the bartender showed me three seed pearls he had taken in payment for some moonshine. He let me hold the pearls, and though they were neither large nor perfectly round, they were beautiful. One was snow-white, another was pink as a sunset, and the third was black and shiny as a speck of coal. I completed my bullhead deliveries on the run so I could get back to my skiff for another try at pearling.

I went for three days without finding a pearl. Then, when the men were out on the river, I found enough courage to approach the woman who stayed in the camp and did the cooking. She looked terribly old, though I don't suppose she was more than forty. She was fat and wore a man's shoes without any socks inside, and though I didn't get close, I could smell moonshine. From a bun on her head, her hair came down in ragged strands like horsehair from an oriole nest that has been in the wind so long it has started unraveling. She was sitting on a stump drinking coffee from a tin cup when I came up, and for a while she just looked at me. I was about to turn and run when she said, "Yes, Boy?"

It was a strangely wonderful voice, deep and throaty. It stopped me in my tracks. Although she had spoken but two words, it came to me at once that she was lonely and beaten and sad. I stared a long time before I realized I was staring. Then, to cover up, I said, "Could I ask you some questions?" I looked down at my feet. I don't suppose I looked up at her once while I was talking. She told me to sit down and asked if I'd like some coffee. I took the coffee. It was so bitter I could hardly swallow it, but I made a pretense of drinking.

After a while she asked, "What do you want to know?" Still looking at my feet, I explained that I wanted to learn how to find pearls. She got up and went to a pile of empty clamshells. A cyclone of flies lifted as she bent over to get one. Then she came back to the stump and told me to watch while she ran her thumbs along each side of the shell under the meat to the spots where the pearls—if there were any—usually lay. In a low, hoarse voice that was almost a whisper, she explained that you had to feel the pearls rather than see them, and that it was even good to shut your eyes while thumbing along beneath the meat so as to be able to

concentrate on the sense of touch.

Then she was silent. After a time, I dared to look into her face and ask, "Is that all there's to it?" She gave her tin cup a toss, and coffee grounds went spraying into a clump of cattails. She looked into the bottom of the cup as though there might be a pearl in it, and then she said, "That's all. That's all that you'd understand." She got up heavily and sighed.

"Thank you," I said, turning away.

Out of the corner of my eye I saw her turn toward me again, so I waited. She put a hand to her face and then said quietly, "Don't thank me, Boy. It's no life, believe me. Forget the pearls. You'll starve trying."

I doubt that I understood at the time what she was trying to say to me, but I waited until she went into the tent. Then I walked as far as it was necessary for politeness before breaking into a gallop.

It wasn't until the next day that I felt the first nubbin beneath my thumb and brought the first seed pearl to the light of day. It was almost as big as a perch's eye, and though not completely round, it had such color as took my breath away. I quickly put it into my mouth, sucked it clean, and then, holding a small medicine bottle to my lips, spit the pearl into it. The pearl shone like captured sunshine, and I just had to sit and marvel at it though every fiber of my being was for getting on with my search for greater riches. I found two smaller ones that day. Even my family was excited by my discovery. We sat around the kerosene lamp until way past my bedtime admiring and talking about the pearls.

After that, there was no time for anything else. My bullhead customers began to complain, my brothers and sisters took to whispering about me, and the fishermen who saw me armpit deep on a bed, feeling for clams with my feet, asked what that crazy kid was up to. I grew lean as a heron. My skin got a leathery look. There were circles under my eyes because I got up so early and was still opening clams long after the mosquitoes had claimed the night as their own.

But when I got back into shoes, to go to school, I had a small wine-glass full of some of the most beautiful pearls a man could ever want to see. I used to spread them on a card table and sit by the hour while the light, like the notes of a song, played a hundred variations on the same theme. None of the pearls was round enough to be worth much money. I knew that, but it made no difference because I didn't want to sell them anyway. Then came the day when I went next door to show the pearls to my grandmother's new boarder. I had spread them on the card table when my dog came running through the room and upset the table. All the pearls went down the large, circular hot-air register of my grandmother's furnace.

I nearly died. And sometimes I think a tiny part of me did. I braved the searing heat and went through the dust and grime that had been accumulating in the old furnace for years, but I never found one of my precious pearls. I figured I had wasted my entire summer, but now that I look back, I know that the summer wasn't wasted. Now I know that the real value was not in the pearls but in the dream. I have never dreamed so grandly since, and I have never come to any adventure with such singleness of purpose. And in losing the pearls, I learned the hardest lesson: All life is transilient. Only the dreams endure.

Mel Ellis

59

At Paul's Pond, in Waukesha County—
George R. Cassidy

X had marked time in the limestone ledge since the Paleozoic seas covered the land. Time, to an atom locked in a rock, does not pass.

The break came when a bur-oak root nosed down a crack and began prying and sucking. In the flash of a century the rock decayed, and X was pulled out and up into the world of living things. He helped build a flower, which became an acorn, which fattened a deer, which fed an Indian, all in a single year.

From his berth in the Indian's bones, X joined again in chase and flight, feast and famine, hope and fear. He felt these things as changes in the little chemical pushes and pulls that tug

Castle Rock, in Castle Rock County Park, Juneau County—Tom Algire

61

Birch reflections—Brian Milne

timelessly at every atom. When the Indian took his leave of the prairie, X moldered briefly underground, only to embark on a second trip through the bloodstream of the land.

This time it was a rootlet of bluestem that sucked him up and lodged him in a leaf that rode the green billows of the prairie June, sharing the common task of hoarding sunlight. To this leaf also fell an uncommon task: flicking shadows across a plover's eggs. The ecstatic plover, hovering overhead, poured praises on something perfect: perhaps the eggs, perhaps the shadows, or perhaps the haze of pink phlox that lay on the prairie.

When the departing plovers set wing for the Argentine, all the bluestems waved farewell with tall new tassels. When the first geese came out of the north and all the bluestems glowed wine-red, a forehanded deermouse cut the leaf in which X lay, and buried it in an underground nest, as if to hide a bit of Indian summer from the thieving frosts. But a fox detained the mouse, molds and fungi took the nest apart, and X lay in the soil again, foot-loose and fancy-free.

Next he entered a tuft of side-oats grama, a buffalo, a buffalo chip, and again the soil. Next a spiderwort, a rabbit, and an owl. Thence a tuft of sporobolus.

All routines come to an end. This one ended with a prairie fire, which reduced the prairie plants to smoke, gas, and ashes. Phosphorus and potash atoms stayed in the ash, but the nitrogen atoms were gone with the wind. A spectator might, at this point, have predicted an early end of the biotic drama, for with fires exhausting the nitrogen, the soil might well have lost its plants and blown away.

But the prairie had two strings to its bow. Fires thinned its grasses, but they thickened its stand of leguminous herbs: prairie clover, bush clover, wild bean, vetch, lead-plant, trefoil, and Baptisia, each carrying its own bacteria housed in nodules on its rootlets. Each nodule pumped nitrogen out of the air into the plant, and then ultimately into the soil. Thus the prairie savings bank took in more nitrogen from its legumes than it paid out to its fires. That the prairie is rich is known to the humblest deermouse; why the prairie is rich is a question seldom asked in all the still lapse of ages.

Blazing stars at the University of Wisconsin Arboretum's Curtis Prairie, in Madison—Bob Jaeger

Between each of his excursions through the biota, X lay in the soil and was carried by the rains, inch by inch, downhill. Living plants retarded the wash by impounding atoms; dead plants by locking them to their decayed tissues. Animals ate the plants and carried them briefly uphill or downhill, depending on whether they died or defecated higher or lower than they fed. No animal was aware that the altitude of his death was more important than his manner of dying. Thus a fox caught a gopher in a meadow, carrying X uphill to his bed on the brow of a ledge, where an eagle laid him low. The dying fox sensed the end of his chapter in foxdom, but not the new beginning in the odyssey of an atom.

An Indian eventually inherited the eagle's plumes, and with them propitiated the Fates, whom he assumed had a special interest in Indians. It did not occur to him that they might be busy casting dice against gravity; that mice and men, soils and songs, might be merely ways to retard the march of atoms to the sea.

One year, while X lay in a cottonwood by the river, he was eaten by a beaver, an animal that always feeds higher than he dies. The beaver starved when his pond dried up during a bitter frost. X rode the carcass down the spring freshet, losing more altitude each hour than heretofore in a century. He ended up in the silt of a backwater bayou, where he fed a crayfish, a coon, and then an Indian, who laid him down to his last sleep in a mound on the riverbank. One spring an oxbow caved the bank, and after one short week of freshet X lay again in his ancient prison, the sea.

An atom at large in the biota is too free to know freedom; an atom back in the sea has forgotten it. For every atom lost to the sea, the prairie pulls another out of the decaying rocks. The only certain truth is that its creatures must suck hard, live fast, and die often, lest its losses exceed its gains.

The Wisconsin River from Cactus Bluff, near Sauk City—Ken Dequaine

64

It is the nature of roots to nose into cracks. When Y was thus released from the parent ledge, a new animal had arrived and begun redding up the prairie to fit his own notions of law and order. An oxteam turned the prairie sod, and Y began a succession of dizzy annual trips through a new grass called wheat.

The old prairie lived by the diversity of its plants and animals, all of which were useful because the sum total of their co-operations and competitions achieved continuity. But the wheat farmer was a builder of categories; to him only wheat and oxen were useful. He saw the useless pigeons settle in clouds upon his wheat, and shortly cleared the skies of them. He saw the chinch bugs take over the stealing job, and fumed because here was a useless thing too small to kill. He failed to see the downward wash of over-wheated loam, laid bare in spring against the pelting rains. When soil-wash and chinch bugs finally put an end to wheat farming, Y and his like had already traveled far down the watershed.

When the empire of wheat collapsed, the settler took a leaf from the old prairie book: he impounded his fertility in livestock, he augmented it with nitrogen-pumping alfalfa, and he tapped the lower layers of the loam with deep-rooted corn.

But he used his alfalfa, and every other new weapon against wash, not only to hold his old plowings, but also to exploit new ones which, in turn, needed holding.

So, despite alfalfa, the black loam grew gradually thinner. Erosion engineers built dams and terraces to hold it. Army engineers built levees and wing-dams to flush it from the rivers. The rivers would not flush, but raised their beds instead, thus choking navigation. So the engineers built pools like gigantic beaver ponds, and Y

West of Sturgeon Bay in Door County—
Ted Laatsch

landed in one of these, his trip from rock to river completed in one short century.

On first reaching the pool, Y made several trips through water plants, fish, and waterfowl. But engineers build sewers as well as dams, and down them comes the loot of all the far hills and the sea. The atoms that once grew pasque-flowers to greet the returning plovers now lie inert, confused, imprisoned in oily sludge.

Roots still nose among the rocks. Rains still pelt the fields. Deermice still hide their souvenirs of Indian summer. Old men who helped destroy the pigeons still recount the glory of the fluttering hosts. Black and white buffalo pass in and out of red barns, offering free rides to itinerant atoms.

Aldo Leopold

On the Manitowish River, between Rest and Stone lakes—Bud Michaelis

Walleyes and other denizens of Vilas County's Sparkling Lake—Douglas R. Stamm

Our beautiful lake, named Fountain Lake by father, but Muir's Lake by the neighbors, is one of the many small glacier lakes that adorn the Wisconsin landscapes. It is fed by twenty or thirty meadow springs, is about half a mile long, half as wide, and surrounded by low finely-modeled hills dotted with oak and hickory, and meadows full of grasses and sedges and many beautiful orchids and ferns. First there is a zone of green, shining rushes, and just beyond the rushes a zone of white and orange water-lilies fifty or sixty feet wide forming a magnificent border. On bright days, when the lake was rippled by a breeze, the lilies and sun-spangles danced together in radiant beauty, and it became difficult to discriminate between them.

On Sundays, after or before chores and sermons and Bible-lessons, we drifted about on the lake for hours, especially in lily time, getting finest lessons and sermons from the water and flowers, ducks, fishes, and muskrats. In particular we took Christ's advice and devoutly "considered the lilies"—how they grow up in beauty out of gray lime mud, and ride gloriously among the breezy sun-spangles. On our way home we gathered grand bouquets of them to be kept fresh all the week. No flower was hailed with greater wonder and admiration by the European settlers in general—Scotch, English, and Irish—than this white water-lily (*Nymphoea odorata*). It is a magnificent plant, queen of the inland waters, pure white, three or four inches in diameter, the most beautiful, sumptuous, and deliciously fragrant of all our Wisconsin flowers. No lily garden in civilization we had ever seen could compare with our lake garden.

John Muir

Wisconsin is a land carved of history and dreams. She remains as a country mystical to some, as though a lodestone drew ancestors to a fulfillment of motherland. Attach to Wisconsin a spirit as gentle as downslope of an easy hill or as spread-across fields of grasses or grains. Her spell is as old as time, for of time and stone and water was Wisconsin created. The lands of Wisconsin were ironed by ice. The tall, blue glaciers distributed the soils, softened the aspects of earth, and sculptured a prophecy of a heartland that would remain over generations as fulfillment of search for peoples of many nations.

Visitors to pioneer Wisconsin described the beautiful and varied horizons; to them the land of Wisconsin seemed the homeland and the paradise they sought. They knew little of the great glaciers that left mixed soils, moraines, and huge marshes where wildfowl nested and fed.

The early settlers, drawn by the lure of the land and the rumors and advertisements that appeared in Europe and in many parts of America, could not interpret the surface of the earth. They did not know that different geologic periods had formed within the state the northern highlands, the Lake Superior lowland, a great central plain, the eastern ridges and lowlands, and in the west a wide, great upland. They did not realize when they first arrived that there was a "driftless area" with odd rock formations that covered western and southwestern Wisconsin, an area the glaciers never touched.

In the glaciated parts the land was fertile, varied, and beautiful, with great timberlands and hundreds of lakes. There were no lakes in the driftless parts and few marshes. The rivers flowed through slowly, almost dreamily, except in flood. Along the Kickapoo, life itself moved quietly.

Robert and Maryo Gard

71

A water lily in a pond northwest of Crivitz, in Marinette County—Jerry Kiesow

In Jackson County—Joseph Fire

Summer is where everybody goes
when June arrives. The journey
generally takes no more effort than to
fall asleep at night between cool sheets
and to awake in the morning with
sunlight pouring like lemonade into the
bedroom, a breeze blowing back the
curtains, and the air feeling the way it
does in the shady part of a lake at
sunrise.

Sunrise in northwoods lake country—
Charles F. Davis

Orb webs in a field near Hartford, in Washington
County—Stephen J. Krasemann

There is no post office at Summer, no school and no time clock. Summer is the hometown of our minds—a place filled with parks, lakes, beaches, climbing trees, bicycles, fishing poles, and baseball bats. There is no charge to get to Summer, but we pay a price nonetheless; the price is the knowledge that our sojourn in the town is shorter with each nightfall.

Go to Summer in excitement, as when you and your friends waited weeks for the Ringling Bros. and Barnum & Bailey Circus to come to town so you could all help put up the tents for free passes. Travel in anticipation, as when you went fishing in pursuit of the smallmouth bass.

Join your children there in childhood, when time stretches ahead in vast, mysterious ebbs and flows, when the fabric of a life is being woven, when there are moments of sublime joy and savage sorrow—and no explanation for either. Remember romance, when you fell in love with practically every girl you met, and some of them fell in love with you.

The Great Midwest Balloon Rally, held annually at Wisconsin Dells—Jon Holtzman

Ride bikes along country lanes. Play baseball during the day and spin-the-bottle at night. Watch a thunderstorm rise over Summer, a towering mass emitting lightning, thunder, and finally rain. Sit on a porch and talk. Lie on the grass and look for four-leaf clovers. Swim in cool water. Dive and don't worry about belly flopping.

Find a home in Summer and stay there until the last dog barks, the last leaf drops, the first snow falls.

Larry Van Goethem

Port Washington's harbor, on Lake Michigan in Ozaukee County—Jerry Kiesow

The Elroy-Sparta State Trail, in Monroe County,
part of Wisconsin's network of bikeways—
Jeff Dean

Lake Michigan and the Cana Island lighthouse, in Door County—Wayne Harmann

The marina at Bayfield, on Lake Superior—Ken Dequaine

The blueness of the waters of the Great Lakes is remarkable; so unlike river water, or the colorless water of our mountain lakes. The vast expanse of the blue sky above them seems to have colored them; the heavenly blue is contagious and affects the water. There is a hint of the sea in the Great Lakes. In the smallest of them that I have seen there is a strange, far-off, elemental look. Superior is the father of it. You feel that that water has been somewhere, and has had unusual experiences.

John Burroughs

Today's family vacationers take their summer house with them—a bus, trailer, camper, or tent. It's fun, of course, after a year stuck in town. Yet some of the Depression generation must dream wistfully of all the quiet, comfortable, old log cabins and cottages now gathering moss north of Rhinelander, Medford, and Eau Claire. Every family had one—rented or inherited—that they returned to year after year. At sunset, you bumped down the last sandy logging road, and there it was—Camp Trail's End, a red tar-paper shack with white battens, a peeled jack-pine flagpole, and Uncle Jake's whitewashed old duck skiff, now full of tiger lilies. You always dashed down the hill and out on the dock for a first look at the clear, green waters of Lake Dorothy while Dad pried off the nailed shutters (swearing once again that he would find a better way in the fall) and Mom hunted the key (always hung inside a floor joist, three studs to the left of the door).

The hand pump in the kitchen had to be primed, the kerosene stove filled, the flypaper strung up, the rag rugs shaken, and the Flit gun sprayed vigorously to discourage flies. Old cottages always smelled, but pleasantly, of a generation of woodsmoke, pipe tobacco, bacon grease, oil of citronella, and mildewed mohair armchairs damp from the spring's roof leaks.

After a quick supper there was just time for a boy to make a few casts from shore, hurling a red-and-white Bass-Oreno with his new Sears, Roebuck telescopic steel casting rod. Inevitably there was a hopeless backlash to unsnarl—picking with a crochet hook in the glow of the bare light-bulb. Then to bed, to fall asleep at last to the slap of pinochle cards and the pop of beer caps.

How glorious to awaken to sunlight pouring through a crack in the eaves, the sight of the blue lake through a grove of white birches. What to do on a morning when Oneida County has become a paradise of clear skies, soft air, and earthy woods smells? There were scratchy wool bathing suits to dig out, embarrassingly holed despite the reeking mothballs in the trunk, and a shocking, cold plunge down to the bright gravel off the cove beach.

Some mornings it rained, of course; gray, sluicing sheets that drummed on the stove flashing. But soon there were fat pine-knots popping in the stove, and pancakes on the table, and the big blue enamel coffeepot exhaling clouds of fragrant glory. What to do with an all-day soaker and whitecaps on the lake? Your mother gazed out the steaming windows, planning an expedition after balsam and sweet fern to stuff the pillows she had embroidered all winter.

A kid could rummage in the bookshelf for the book he'd been reading last Labor Day, *The Bobbsey Twins' Adventure in the Country*. He and his sister could play old maid or get out the jigsaw puzzle of the moose and hunter—the box carefully marked "five pieces missing" so you wouldn't go crazy looking for pieces to complete the waterfall behind the moose. He could sit at the round oak table and study the camp's museum of wonders, ranging from the German steel helmet Uncle Jake brought back from Saint-Mihiel (with a frightening bullet hole added for effect) to dried shelf mushrooms painted with Indian warbonnets and "Souvenir of

82

Minocqua, 1932."

Your father and your uncle Ivan eyed the horseshoes pit, calculating that by evening the wind might lay enough to seine minnows and try for a mess of walleyes off Link's Point. After twenty-five years, they knew every sandbar and weed bed in the lake, just where to get lunkers like those whose gaping, snaggletoothed heads were nailed to trees around the fish-cleaning bench. About twice a summer they borrowed a pickup truck and horsed a boat into Sweeney Lake, sworn to hold the world's record muskie. ("Chet Boynton says the conservation boys netted it through the ice in '28— seventy-four pounds!") And there were pudgy, black bluegills to catch, too, yanked from the lily pads with a cane pole, cork bobber, and pink curl of night crawler.

Not that it was all straw-hat fun. The wooden rowboats always leaked and had to be bailed with a squashed lard can. Sometimes you even had to take a bath in the lake, using a red, carbolicky bar of Lifebuoy that would turn a bass belly-up at ten yards. But these were also the days when ecology was only a gleam in the eye of a cranky Madison professor named Leopold.

And so it went in those simple, peaceful days—waves lapping against the dock, a phoebe nesting in the woodshed, a black iron skillet frying perch to a crispness unknown to Teflon, the hoot of the Flambeau 400 pounding north through the dark forest for Ashland and Lake Superior.

Jay Scriba

Indian pipes in Wisconsin's northwoods— Jerry Kiesow

Devils Lake, in northern Vilas County— Ken Dequaine

I toss sleepless in the August night, watching the cat pant in the window after another 90-degree day. Glowing clock hands insist that it is midnight, yet who can tell with brassy new streetlights banishing even the moonlight to the darkest alleys.

It is a haunting hour when, for me, hooting old factory whistles unreel visions of Ellis Island in the dawn, immigrant fathers with lunch buckets, jars of Warsaw pickles in cellars along Mitchell Street. Without thinking about it, I find myself up and dressed, walking the beagle on sidewalks still warm from the western sun.

For the nature watcher, a summer midnight in the city is most striking for what is missing. There are no whippoorwills in the elm tops, no fireflies sparking in the lilac bushes, no bullfrogs trumping, no mosquitoes whining in your ears. There is no hovering owl, although I keep hoping that St. John's Cathedral tower will one day attract a pair of the goggle-eyed barn owls that like such nesting places. There is no green fox-fire in the shadows, no brush wolf yipping on the hill.

Yet even in the heart of the city the cat's swishing tail speaks of fluttering moth wings at the screen, of small furry scurryings in the weed patch across the way. Bats and chimney swifts still swirl like gnats above the yellow gas weather flame. Nighthawks beep and swoosh high in the dark, above the blazing downtown canyons. There is a banging of garbage cans back in an alley where, for an instant, the sly face of a thieving raccoon peers at me like some masked troll.

On the Kilbourn Avenue median, a young cottontail rabbit quits nibbling clover, frozen by the red lights and sudden siren of a speeding police car. In the woodsy grove of Cathedral

Square, there are night crawlers oozing in the grass and two boys hunting them with flashlights. Pausing at curbside, I am pleased to hear the sleepy chirp of a resident cricket.

My friend Tom, the glassblower, insists that "Milwaukee has only seven stars" compared to the thousands that sparkle in the clear air over his Door County farm. Tonight it may be true, with a milky ground haze tasting of burned gasoline, rancid frying pans, and much-breathed air.

In the silence you can hear an electric hum in the tunnel under the sidewalk, a thick gurgling beneath a manhole cover. Near the home block a rat scoots across a street shining with flattened wads of chewing gum from the corner drugstore. Brawling tomcats hiss and spit in their parking-lot arena. Pigeons blink from the gingerbread on the Civil War boarding house that is

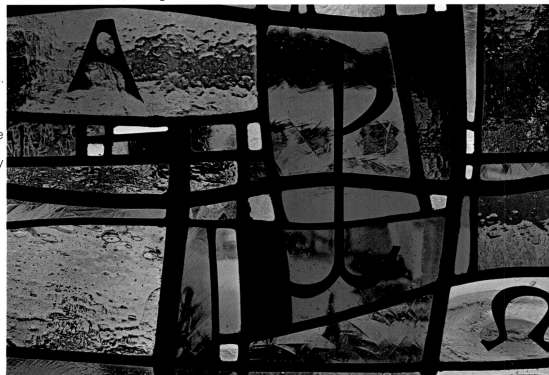

Milwaukee, America's stained-glass capital—courtesy of Conrad Schmitt Studios, Milwaukee

Downtown Madison—Bruce Fritz

Sunset over Lake Monona and the Madison
skyline—David Gilbert

their historic roosting place. A damp, fish-smelling breeze puffs in off Lake Michigan, cooling the plaza around the fountain splashing in Cathedral Square.

As the moon glides white and high, the city seems deserted except for its moths, nighthawks, and four-footed prowlers. Yet it remains overwhelmingly a place of mankind, with vigil candles behind the cathedral's stained glass, with a lighted window or two marking some pleasure or misery on the cliff face of a Juneau Village high rise.

The beagle whines and tugs at the leash as we pass air-conditioners whirring with the ghostly energy of plants and animals dead one hundred million years. And there, almost straight up, is the brightest of Tom's precious seven—the glittering white eye of Vega, which may still be watching when the blue-green ball of Earth fades into its final night.

Jay Scriba

Along the Namekagon River—Richard H. Smith, Earth Imagery

Autumn

A ruffed grouse—Brian Milne

The ruffed grouse lurk in the river bottoms where spruce and cedar grow out of wet black earth. The birds drum up in front of hunters, just a heartbeat ahead of the shotgun pellets that reach for them. Overhead, the geese are flying south again, flocks stretched out in the sky, rising and falling in the rhythm of wing, day, month, year, era.

The bright promise of the new autumn has given slow way to the first freezes. Yet the woods smell sweet with the fragrance of October: a perfume of puffballs—earth's ferment in the humus—drying leaves, and torn cobwebs. A haze lies upon the countryside, and there is a faint smell of smoke in the air. The neon signs of nature, the sugar maples, still flash brightly with red and orange. It is Indian summer.

Larry Van Goethem

We called it Mushroom Hill, but it was really a succession of kettles and eskers, bare-branched woods, and a cow pasture. It was a Waukesha County dairy farm that my family visited during the autumn months. In the spring of my life.

It was the mushrooms that drew us there, especially the chunky-shanked *Boletus aurantiacus,* its russet caps crowded together like miniature umbrellaed burghers; and graceful *Boletus mirabilis,* with elongated teardrop stems, fragile to the touch. During those green-golden years of my youth, the high point of the autumn months was a day at Mushroom Hill. Autumn was gathering time, mushroom-hunting time, and the hunt was rich with rewards.

It began with an hour-long drive along tire-thumping dirt roads that etched the countryside. It depended on a bachelor farmer in bib overalls, who enjoyed an earnest conversation with my parents concerning crops and cattle. It continued with a childhood fear of grazing cows in a pasture that had to be crossed, and the rough reassurance of a father's embrace. And then there was the smell of picnic coffee. Picnic coffee was coffee *ordinaire* until it was drunk in an open field on a brittle sunlit November noon, which immediately made it a magical brew. I remember the sinful practice of prying shards of bark from the shagbark hickory tree, the sight of plum-purple storm clouds roiling the north sky, sere leaves deep enough to cover my boot tops, the musky smell of earth, the sting of a wind-whipped face, and an endless exultation known as boyhood.

94

Near Caroline, in Shawano County—
Ken Dequaine

Milking time—William E. Ruth

Holy Hill and a Catholic shrine, in Washington County—William Lawrence Stonecipher

Once, urged on by an older and adventurous sister, I toiled to drag an abandoned farm cart to the crest of a precipitous hill. Having triumphed over the slope, we paused to savor the expectation of what was to follow. Then, with hoarse screams, we pushed the wheels down the slope. Down the imaginary canyon road they raced—the runaway steeds foam-flecked, the cart (a stagecoach) caroming off boulders, scything brittle stalks of Indian tobacco, leaping a gully, and coming to a wonderfully abrupt, splintering stop against an unyielding crab-apple tree.

I scrambled into the drooping arms of the old tree, dangled my feet, and teased the wind-tossed leaves to leap up and dislodge me. And though they swirled and darted and clung to my brown fuzzy scarf with their serrated edges, they could not. Then it was a downward leap out of the tree, a scramble on hands and feet, a headlong rush over the next hill in an open-mouthed race against myself. Gaining the top, I stopped, suddenly immobile at the sight of my father kneeling.

I watched in silence. From the host roots of a corrugated hickory stump he delicately excised a cluster of tiny mushrooms. I could not decide whether his concentration dwelt on the mysterious microcosm of the spore or on a gourmet anticipation of the mushrooms simmering in sauces, bathing in soups. But there was a solemnity to the scene that made me sidle away, sensing I had intruded on a personal ritual.

For me, there were more hills to conquer, more acorns and hickory nuts with which to bulge my pockets. There were chipmunks to be harassed, a stone fence whose length had to be walked, a neighboring cornfield needing investigation. Then I returned to the rolling stone-dotted hills, back into the outstretched branches of the woods. I ran and I ran and I ran. And the elders knelt.

The mushroom hunt continued

throughout the afternoon, and at day's end it always stormed. The wind took on an icy push and hurried us off the land. It hastened us out of the hills and into the farmyard, flayed the farewells from our mouths and merged them with the rush of its own voice. It forced us to the car, where, gasping from the cold and a nervous fear of the motor not starting, we sat and noisily exhaled white vapor. During the drive home, I covered myself with the car robe, dozed, and asked repeatedly if we

Elm logs and fungi in Madison—David Gilbert

98

In Polk County—Tom Algire

would return the following weekend.

The Waukesha County farm still exists, having thus far escaped the subdivider's transit. The farmer has long since departed. The mushrooms are still there, I'm sure, but the hills appear to brood, as though yearning for the harmonies of an Old World understanding of the land.

Raymond Helminiak

Weeds, a friend says, are only flowers growing where you did not plant them. Along the hedges, in the fencerow, and even in the garden corners where cultivation flagged with the waning season, the New England aster showers blue sparks in affirmation. This wildflower—or weed, if you will—is my favorite among a tribe that must number two hundred species, though the common garden annual is not among them.

Aster means "star" in Latin, hence some classicists still call the family starwort, and the plant is a relative of goldenrod and fleabane. But you do not need to know these things to admire the proud barbarians blooming in the hedge. In its natural habits, the aster is too bold and brash for gardens. Its leaves are rough in your fingers, and it grows five feet high in good ground. It is a hairy, sticky, rude fellow, elbowing even ragweed aside to gain the light, but its flowers are a disciplined praise of autumn. These flowers may range in hue from white to pink to darkest violet. Mine are vivid blue, an inch and a half across, with good gold centers among the delicate frieze of ray flowers.

Like all composites, asters make fruit, thus adding to the larder that the hedge produces. This is of interest to foraging mice and small birds, for whom the tall dry stalks will offer a harvest even in deep snow, but it does not concern me personally; it has nothing to do with the feeling of welcome recognition that comes with the opening of the first bright clusters.

I do not know why it should be so, but if the New England aster must go in order that I should have a clean garden, then I will not have a clean garden. If I must endure burdock and ragweed to keep the aster, then I will sneeze in payment. And I will regard the spraddled holdout in the hedge as a stubborn sermon against the deathly sanitation of wide-spectrum herbicides. There are some problems in the green world, as in others, where solution, however ready, comes at too high a price.

Dion Henderson

Asters at Rock Island State Park—Ken Dequaine

We were paddling northward, Dad and I, through a slate-gray morning in canoe country. As we approached a narrows midway up the lake, rain swished down from the north to meet us. In the heart of the narrows, sheer walls of rock, splashed with surrealistic orange and a strange blue, plunged down from great height. I was peering through this canyon, eager for the sight of the main body of the lake, when I saw something far ahead on the water. I beckoned to Dad. "Something's up ahead," I half whispered. We rested paddles and looked into the slanting rain.

It was only a lone beaver, swimming our way. But we sat tight, drifting in the gusts of wind that bullied through the cliffs. We were curious to see how close he'd come before he smacked the water with his tail and dived. But onward he swam, bearing down on us without a waver. Excitement began to swell inside of me as the solitary swimmer steadily narrowed the gap between us. He was bigger than any beaver I'd ever seen. And he was old.

Finally, a paddle's length off the bow, he paused in confusion. He turned in an uneasy half circle, then hung in the water as though waiting for us to make the next move. All at once he lunged upward in strange desperation, pointing his snout directly at me. I looked at his scarred old head and at his eyes. And then I understood. The milky eyes peered at me with a transparent stare. "He's blind!" I said. But the wind tore my words away. Silently, we watched him turn away and thread his sightless course down the narrows. Small whitecaps now and then sloshed up to blot him from view. At last he faded into the curtain of rain.

The wind, though dying, still tormented the pines as we sat by our

Portaging over a beaver dam on the Manitowish River—Jeff Dean

Fallen leaves of birch and maple—Glenn Van Nimwegen ·

Following spread: Lake Superior at the mouth of the Bois Brule River—Bruce Fritz

campfire that night. I huddled beside the flames—a speck of light in a sea of darkness—seeking a warmth I couldn't find.

"Tough break for that beaver to lose its sight," Dad said. I nodded, staring into the fire. "But he's still making out," Dad went on. "Still got his other senses and his strength. Notice how he kept his head up and swam right on? That's courage!"

Dad could sense my fear and confusion. "Nature's so far beyond us, son, that we'll never be able to understand all her ways. Like that beaver, we're all here to shift pretty much for ourselves. That's the way it has to be, for free beings."

As Dad talked on quietly, the wind whispered down into silence, and the stars came out. Wisps of reconciliation began to come, began to mingle with my fear and confusion, began to drive away some of the oppression. As I lay in my blankets I thought of the sightless beaver, remembering the stony stare, wondering where he was out there in the blackness, wondering how he would fare when winter came snarling over the lakes and hills.

In the succeeding days and months the milky eyes appeared often to haunt me, especially before I dropped off to sleep at night. They were pleading for help, asking for guidance through those rugged narrows, through the wilderness, through a starkly solitary life. But gradually the jagged edges of the memory began to smooth down in the incessant flow of time. I came to think less of the milky eyes, and more of the way the creature had forged stoically on to vanish in the rain. I came to sense a greatness in it, a wild freedom, an unflinching courage.

Today, looking back upon that youthful experience, I still feel a faint twinge. But I also feel the inexpressible emotion that rushes over you when you suddenly come upon a new lake and stand in the wind on the wild shore, gazing into the mighty, bluish sweep where the whitecaps are breaking crisp and clean. Somehow, that same kind of wind-swept bigness is in it, mingled with a soaring thankfulness for life—with all its risk and opportunity, its unseen promises of tragedy or joy, its unknown tomorrow of darkness or splendid light.

Phil Carspecken

A beaver lodge on the Red Cliff Indian Reservation, in Bayfield County—Ken Dequaine

The west bluff view at Devils Lake State Park—Bob Jaeger

I love Wisconsin's small towns, the air of the bucolic that exists just outside Milwaukee. I love the names of the towns, like Tomahawk, Colfax, Pound, Footville, Hurley. I love the Wisconsin of town halls, shuttered country churches—steeples rising on prairie horizons—and barns and silos looming in the Kettle Moraine.

I visited New York City once and thought I was in a foreign country. And when I came back to Wisconsin, it was as a native to the hearth.

Larry Van Goethem

A produce stand at Burkhardt, in St. Croix County—R. S. Hedin

The Wisconsin Idea is a term that has had and still has both national and international currency. Indeed, in 1952, the Democratic nominee for the presidency of the United States characterized it as one of the truly creative ideas of the twentieth century. Others both before and since have spoken as rapturously about it. In 1912 Frederick C. Howe declared that Wisconsin was "an experiment station in politics, in social and industrial legislation, in the democratization of science and higher education."

It would probably be impossible to get complete agreement on a detailed statement of what the Wisconsin Idea embraced, even in 1912, but many persons would agree that experimental reform based upon detailed research, the extensive use of academic and other experts in government, agriculture, and industry, and an enlightened electorate were all prominent elements. Some observers might explain the origin of the Wisconsin Idea wholly in terms of the work and personalities of men like Robert M. La Follette, Sr., leader of the progressive Republicans in Wisconsin for a quarter of a century, and Charles R. Van Hise, President of the University from 1903 to 1918. Others might insist that geography would explain it. The Capitol and the main University building are located just one mile apart, each standing on its respective section corner. State Street, laid out along the section line, connects what William Ellery Leonard called the "twin domes of law and learning."

That a state-supported university should contribute directly to improved farming, more efficient industry, and better government was not a new idea in the United States even when the University of Wisconsin was created in 1848. But it was one thing to propose such a program; it was quite another thing to do something about it.

In 1887 Thomas C. Chamberlin came to the University as president. Chamberlin was a man of originality and boldness and his mind was unfettered by commitment to any one type of learning or one discipline as the single road to educational salvation. On one occasion he declared: "Scholarship for the sake of the scholar is simply refined selfishness. Scholarship for the sake of the state and the people is refined patriotism." In 1891 a program of general University extension courses was inaugurated.

During the first year it was estimated that some 8,500 people attended these lectures. Interest continued during the next few years, and in the middle 1890's President C. K. Adams, who had succeeded Chamberlin in 1892, reported that various reform movements had been launched in some communities as a result of the University extension lectures.

At this juncture several important events occurred. Robert M. La Follette was elected to the governorship in 1900. Of the University, he said: "For myself, I owe what I am and what I have done largely to the inspiration I received while there." In 1903 Charles R. Van Hise became President of the University. In his inaugural address Van Hise proposed that professors be used as technical experts by the state government. He felt that professors had knowledge that might be useful in helping to solve social and political problems. Nor did he propose in vain. Governor La Follette had already begun to use them in state positions.

The fact that University professors were advising the governor and the Legislature and serving in administrative and other posts in the state government presented a novelty certain to be commented upon by reporters sent to spy out La Follette's state. Equally important was the revival of University extension work. In 1905 Van Hise declared to the Regents: "Too much cannot be said as to the importance of University extension under which the University goes out to the people."

The frank dedication of the University to service and the lines the service took won enthusiastic acclaim. In 1909 Lincoln Steffens published an article in the *American Magazine* entitled, "Sending a State to College." A year later E. E. Slosson declared that "it is impossible to ascertain the size or location of the University of Wisconsin. The most that one can say is that the headquarters of the institution is at the city of Madison and that the campus has an area of about 56,000 square miles."

Many observers thought they saw, beyond the courses in sanitary sewerage, highway construction, and shop mathematics offered by the Extension Division, the promise of a new, completely informed, progressive America. All of these elements, the large program of legislative reform, the expert work of the professors, the work of the Legislative Reference Library, the vigorous extension work of the University, and the staunch devotion of the University to the principle that the professors should be untrammeled in their pursuit of truth, were part of the Wisconsin Idea. The mark of that Idea is still on the state and nation.

Vernon Carstensen

Madison, Wisconsin's capital city—Doug Wollin,
Wollin Studios; courtesy of Madison City
Planning Department

Wilderness is the raw material out of which man has hammered the artifact called civilization.

Wilderness was never a homogeneous raw material. It was very diverse, and the resulting artifacts are very diverse. These differences in the end-product are known as cultures. The rich diversity of the world's cultures reflects a corresponding diversity in the wilds that gave them birth.

For the first time in the history of the human species, two changes are now impending. One is the exhaustion of wilderness in the more habitable portions of the globe. The other is the world-wide hybridization of cultures through modern transport and industrialization. Neither can be prevented, and perhaps should not be, but the question arises whether, by some slight amelioration of the impending changes, certain values can be preserved that would otherwise be lost.

To the laborer in the sweat of his labor, the raw stuff on his anvil is an adversary to be conquered. So was wilderness an adversary to the pioneer.

But to the laborer in repose, able for the moment to cast a philosophical eye on his world, that same raw stuff is something to be loved and cherished, because it gives definition and meaning to his life. This is a plea for the preservation of some tag-ends of wilderness, as museum pieces, for the edification of those who may one day wish to see, feel, or study the origins of their cultural inheritance.

113

The Amnicon River at Amnicon Falls State Park, in Douglas County—Jeff Dean

In the Northern Unit of the Kettle Moraine State
Forest—Ted Rosenbaum

Many of the diverse wildernesses out of which we have hammered America are already gone; hence in any practical program the unit areas to be preserved must vary greatly in size and in degree of wildness.

No living man will see again the long-grass prairie, where a sea of prairie flowers lapped at the stirrups of the pioneer. We shall do well to find a forty here and there on which the prairie plants can be kept alive as species. There were a hundred such plants, many of exceptional beauty. Most of them are quite unknown to those who have inherited their domain.

But the short-grass prairie, where Cabeza de Vaca saw the horizon under the bellies of the buffalo, is still extant in a few spots of 10,000-acre size, albeit severely chewed up by sheep, cattle, and dry-farmers. If the forty-niners are worth commemorating on the walls of state capitols, is not the scene of their mighty hegira worth commemorating in several national prairie reservations?

No living man will see again the virgin pineries of the Lake States, or the flatwoods of the coastal plain, or the giant hardwoods; of these, samples of a few acres each will have to suffice. But there are still several blocks of maple-hemlock of thousand-acre size; there are similar blocks of Appalachian hardwoods, of southern hardwood swamp, of cypress swamp, and of Adirondack spruce. Few of these tag-ends are secure from prospective cuttings, and fewer still from prospective

Asters—Stephen J. Krasemann

tourist roads.

One of the fastest-shrinking categories of wilderness is coastlines. Cottages and tourist roads have all but annihilated wild coasts on both oceans, and Lake Superior is now losing the last large remnant of wild shoreline on the Great Lakes. No single kind of wilderness is more intimately interwoven with history, and none nearer the point of complete disappearance.

———————

Physical combat for the means of subsistence was, for unnumbered centuries, an economic fact. When it disappeared as such, a sound instinct led us to preserve it in the form of athletic sports and games.

Physical combat between man and beasts was, in like manner, an economic fact, now preserved as hunting and fishing for sport.

Public wilderness areas are, first of all, a means of perpetuating, in sport form, the more virile and primitive skills in pioneering travel and subsistence.

Some of these skills are of generalized distribution; the details have been adapted to the American scene, but the skill is world-wide. Hunting, fishing, and foot travel by pack are examples.

Two of them, however, are as American as a hickory tree; they have been copied elsewhere, but they were developed to their full perfection only on this continent. One of these is canoe travel, and the other is travel by

Douglas County's Lake Superior shoreline—
Bruce Fritz

pack-train. Both are shrinking rapidly. Your Hudson Bay Indian now has a put-put, and your mountaineer a Ford. If I had to make a living by canoe or packhorse, I should likely do likewise, for both are grueling labor. But we who seek wilderness travel for sport are foiled when we are forced to compete with mechanized substitutes. It is footless to execute a portage to the tune of motor launches, or to turn out your bell-mare in the pasture of a summer hotel. It is better to stay home.

118 Wilderness areas are first of all a series of sanctuaries for the primitive arts of wilderness travel, especially canoeing and packing.

I suppose some will wish to debate whether it is important to keep these primitive arts alive. I shall not debate it. Either you know it in your bones, or you are very, very old.

———

Wilderness is a resource which can shrink but not grow. Invasions can be arrested or modified in a manner to keep an area usable either for recreation, or for science, or for wildlife, but the creation of new wilderness in the full sense of the word is impossible.

It follows, then, that any wilderness program is a rearguard action, through which retreats are reduced to a minimum. The Wilderness Society was organized in 1935 'for the one purpose of saving the wilderness remnants in America.' The Sierra Club is doing yeoman work toward the same end.

It does not suffice, however, to have a few such societies, nor can one be content that Congress has enacted a bill aimed at wilderness preservation. Unless there be wilderness-minded men scattered through all the conservation bureaus, the societies may never learn of new invasions until the time for action has passed. Furthermore, a militant minority of wilderness-minded citizens must be on watch throughout the nation and vigilantly available for action.

In Europe, where wilderness has now retreated to the Carpathians and Siberia, every thinking conservationist bemoans its loss. Even in Britain, which has less room for land-luxuries than almost any other civilized country, there is a vigorous if belated movement for saving a few small spots of semi-wild land.

Ability to see the cultural value of wilderness boils down, in the last analysis, to a question of intellectual humility. The shallow-minded modern who has lost his rootage in the land assumes that he has already discovered what is important; it is such who prate of empires, political or economic, that will last a thousand years. It is only the scholar who appreciates that all history consists of successive excursions from a single starting-point, to which man returns again and again to organize yet another search for a durable scale of values. It is only the scholar who understands why the raw wilderness gives definition and meaning to the human enterprise.

Aldo Leopold

The Bois Brule River, in the Brule River State Forest—Fred Morgan

At the Leopold Memorial Reserve, in Columbia County—Charles Steinhacker, Nature Photography of America

An evergreen-hardwood forest, common in
northern Wisconsin—Tom Algire

Southwestern Wisconsin is as old as the hills of Bethlehem. When you go partridge hunting there, you get a special sense of the Christmas peace that passes understanding. While the rest of the Great Lakes states were being racked and torn in the grip of the great glacier that swept down over the North American continent at the close of the last Ice Age, the so-called Driftless Area of southwest Wisconsin, some two hundred miles long and half as many wide, escaped entirely the avalanche of snow and boulders. Alone, out of all the northern states, this region remained unglaciated, probably because a giant mountain range warded off the monstrous advance. So southwest Wisconsin's terrain bears no battle scars. No lakes were dredged, no hills leveled, no drumlins staked out, no valleys filled in, no streams plugged. Here in a stretch of hills and coulees is an example, discounting the weathering since, of what America looked like before the great glacier pockmarked her face.

Most of the area was once sea bottom. Because the hills escaped the glacier's whittling, the rock records of that strange marine age are still preserved, and wherever the layers of surface soil have been washed away, the records are plainly visible. The creek banks are virtual historical libraries. Showing in bold outline are the skeletons of fish with odd armored heads (the only vertebrates of their time), snail and clam shells, fossil seaweed, and the delicate scrollwork of carboniferous ferns—a veritable textbook of paleontology, inscribed eons ago.

Sandstone castles and mural escarpments punctuate the skyline. Springs gush forth from the great maws of grotesque crags. Hidden valleys provide food and cover for birds. While you pick up your partridge, you find a deeper satisfaction in merely knowing

you are tramping a region geologically
unduplicated on the continent, as
pristine as Galilee.

On the mesas of southwest
Wisconsin a lush growth of bluegrass
flourishes in the limy, sea-distilled soil
and supports an equally lush growth of
beef cattle. But back in the hills the
farming comes hard. Slopes too steep
for corn and even for cows have been
allowed to revert to oak-hickory woods,
interspersed with grape tangles,
sprawling cedar, and old drumming
logs. Cash crops and farmsteads are
lean here, but the ruffed grouse finds a
way to piece together an existence
denied him in more progressive
surroundings. This great native
American game-bird seems to feel
particularly at home in the southwest,
jumping with a roar out of an ancient
conifer or wheeling silently over the
crest of a razorback to drop out of
sight into an eroded canyon.

It is the stage setting that really
gets you. To cruise these preglacial
hills and to know that everything
around and underneath has been from
prehistoric times as unaltered as the
stars overhead—this gives ballast to
minds adrift on change. You can catch,
if you will, in the haze of these
mellowing hills, a glimpse of eternity. It
may bear a striking resemblance to the
tail feathers of a grouse disappearing
fast down the corridors of a timeless
forest.

Clay Schoenfeld

A cross-country skier at Telemark Ski Area, near
Cable—Charles Steinhacker, Nature
Photography of America

Winter

When I was a young skier living in Madison, in the days before I could make a turn to the left, *skiing* meant ski jumping. The only occasion for a turn was to avoid running into the spectators at the bottom of a jumping hill or into the barricades erected to protect the spectators from jumpers who couldn't turn. In those days, waxing skis was individual witchcraft and was performed behind locked doors on the morning before a jumping event. The objective was the fastest possible sliding surface. Each skier would sneak outside, check the temperature, look at the clouds, sniff the air, feel the snow, mutter an incantation (preferably in Norwegian), and return to his hotel room, there to secure the door and apply his own secret formula of the day—which, I discovered later, was always orange shellac. I still associate the aroma of wood alcohol with the excitement of tournament day.

As cross-country racing became popular, waxing became more complex. Those with a near-frictionless surface were left running in place at the starting line while those who had bare boards walked away and those who had discovered beeswax *ran* away.

At about this time my two brothers, Dave and Steve, went to Dartmouth and began to write amazing letters home. They reported that they had learned to make turns to the left and that they had a ski coach named Otto Schniebs who made the most marvelous cross-country waxes. The formulas, of course, were secret, but Otto was turning out cross-country champions.

When Dave and Steve came home from Dartmouth for Christmas, we went up on a wooded hill in Eagle Heights, and they skied down it. But they did not ski in the carefully chosen straight line and at the hair-raising velocities familiar to ski jumpers; they actually turned rhythmically right and left, never once hitting any of the fine big oaks growing there. It took our breath away.

Later I visited Dartmouth and met Otto Schniebs. It was not the most auspicious meeting. I inadvertently walked into his shop while he was in the act of mixing a caldron of his most famous top-secret cross-country wax—Sohm's Blue. He looked up, startled, as I entered, then frowned and growled something in Austrian. Though the words were unfamiliar, the meaning was clear. I left, but not before I'd smelled the hot pine-tar and noticed Otto's left hand full of broken Victrola records about to be tossed into the caldron.

Sohm's Blue was a truly marvelous racing wax. Judiciously applied and under the right weather and snow conditions, Sohm's Blue gave you a feeling of kinship with an impala as you waltzed along the trail to the strains of something by Strauss, switched on by your brain as suitable incidental music for the activity. Modern biological research suggests that the music in your brain resulted from inhaling a few parts per billion of a pheromone emanating from those Austrian Victrola records on the bottom of your skis.

It was World War II and my assignment to the 10th Mountain Division that broadened my vision of skiing and gave me an opportunity to learn left turns under the tutelage of some of Otto Schnieb's disciples. During my first year of military training I worked for the Mountain and Winter Warfare Board, testing clothing, equipment, and rations. One glorious winter day, using skis with mohair climbers, I was padding my way up the final slope below Alta Vista on Mount Rainier when I heard behind me the sound of an approaching skier. The rhythmic breathing well coordinated with the slap-slap of skis told of efficient balance between oxygen intake and energy output. I knew, without bothering to look, that behind me was a mountain man. Soon he pulled out of my track and moved alongside. He was a compact, springy-looking person with bright eyes, small muscular hands, and an air that suggested he did not wholly believe in human equality.

His glance flicked over my skis. "Ha!" he said, smiling. "Vat kind uff vax are you using?" That was rhetorical; he could easily see that I was wearing climbers, and I could easily see that he was coming straight up a twenty-five-degree slope on wax alone, his ski poles tucked under his arms. "I'm trying out a new ski vax for the Army," he said. With that he stomped his skis and took off down the slope in a cloud of powder.

That was my introduction to Fritz Wiessner and his Wonder Red wax. The demonstration was impressive. Ultimately the Army bought a lot of that wax for the ski troops, among whom it became known as Veesner's Vunder Vax. There was no need for the Mountain and Winter Warfare Board to go into an elaborate test program. Sohm's Blue not being available in sufficient quantity, Wiessner's was easily the best wax for the job. But as a former tester, I carried thereafter a hankering to compare Sohm's Blue with Wiessner's Wonder Red.

I emerged from the war a confirmed ski-tourer and a lover of the great white slopes. And over the years, as I observed the veritable avalanche of touring and racing waxes hitting the shelves of sporting-goods stores, my irrational desire to test waxes—the new against the old, the old against each

Skis for rent at Telemark Ski Area, near Cable—
Charles Steinhacker, Nature Photography of
America

other—was reawakened. When I retired and returned to live in Wisconsin, I finally found the time, the place, and of course the snow. Oddly enough, I also found the waxes. I had absconded with a box of Wonder Red when the war ended. And when I moved to Baraboo I uncovered my prewar hoard of Sohm's Blue. It looked ancient, slightly granular and crystalline, but it applied nicely to the bottom of a warm wooden ski and seemed to have kept much of its original quality. And so at last I was able to complete my test.

Here, for general edification, are my conclusions.

● For air temperatures from 30°F down to 10°F on medium granular snow, Sohm's Blue is still king of the racing waxes.

● Sohm's Blue also smells better than any other wax, new or old—if you like the odor of pine tar.

● Icing, however, is a Sohm's Blue problem. Once started, it is hard to correct in the field. In fact, it is difficult to make *any* adjustment to a Sohm's Blue surface in the field.

● Wiessner's Wonder Red generally outperforms all others as a field wax. It exhibits its good qualities over more than the combined temperature range of modern Blue, Green, and Special Green waxes, and seems to have fewer "bugs" than contemporary products.

● Wonder Red also has a fine delicate bouquet—if you like the smell of beeswax.

Modern waxes have no fragrance at all! No alcohol, no pine tar, no beeswax; no scent or waltzing pheromone to catch you unawares in later life and pull you back to the good old days. Pity!

Charles C. Bradley

128

At Telemark Ski Area—Tom Kelly

130

The Kinnickinnic River, near River Falls—
Louis E. Ulrich, Jr.

Walk out into falling snow, the soft, clinging flakes, and be lost and enclosed in an intimate private world by a natural phenomenon that borrows a little from the secret self and a little more from the fundamental mystery of the universe. The world of falling snow is related to that primitive awareness of concealment, which is always accompanied by an acceptance of and a desire to be hidden, akin to being enclosed by night and darkness. Here rather, it is not by darkness but by light, encurtained, as it were, from everything which had been but briefly before familiar and known.

Nothing in this white world is known, every familiar thing appears in strange guise; its inhabitants are creatures but briefly seen existing on a plane of equality with man as seldom at

The Bad River at Copper Falls State Park, in Ashland County—Jeff Dean

any other time—the foraging mouse, the resting deer, the darting rabbit, the industrious nuthatch. Trees looming over are spectral, no longer clearly defined; the sky is an infinity retreating, out of which the flakes descend in an endless cascade; you are in a cocoon of snow, and the prosaic everyday world is shut away.

And the silence! There is nothing equivalent to the silence of snow; all sound in the heart of a snowfall is muffled, distant, as unreal as the world beyond the wall of white. This too is an integral part of the falling snow, a world made up of silence, the endlessly falling flakes, the white strangeness, all lending a sense of the impermanence of things, of the alien within the confines of the known world, a kind of pleasant, reassuring strangeness, since you know that the familiar world lies just under the white blanket, just beyond the fall of flakes, just past the enclosing whiteness.

The backward flight to the womb, the return to the primitive urgence for wariness and concealment from the countless enemies of man's ancestors on the planet, the indulgence in the sense of solitude common to all men, the simple delight in the kind of beauty only a falling snow clinging to blade and leaf, to stone and man alike can afford—perhaps in one or all these lies the secret of this pleasure a man takes in being enclosed and locked away from the mundane world of every day by the intimate white flakes of this private world.

August Derleth

In Manitowoc County—Dorothy Bugs

Along Menomonee River Parkway, in Milwaukee—Greg Puza

134

My wife and I claim the new world record: Taking turns on the sidewalk, we kicked a three-inch chunk of ice for ten blocks, including up and down curbs (the hard part), and even across the Wisconsin Avenue bridge. We started at our East Side flat and finally crushed the last skittering fragment in front of Buddy Squirrel's Nut Shop (which some may see as appropriate).

Throughout, however, I felt guilty, because ice is not a substance to be kicked around by ungrateful humans. Rather, we should sprinkle libations to the water sprites for ensuring that, unlike other fluids, water expands when it freezes. Thus ice floats. Thus it does not sink to the bottoms of our rivers, lakes, and oceans, accumulating to transform the world into one big frozen Ellesmere land.

Although large masses of ice are classed scientifically as rock, some few scholars have argued that it is alive and, indeed, demonstrates a mechanical basis for all life. One of these became so fascinated by the way ice crystals multiply that he crowned his life's work with a book entitled *The Souls of Crystals*.

Thoreau, on a sunny March morning, thought he could see the primordial formation of human veins, arteries, and capillaries in the melting lobes and tricklets of ice in a sand cut on the Fitchburg railway.

"What is man but a mass of thawing clay?" he wrote in *Walden*. "The ball of the human finger is but a drop congealed. The chin is a still larger drop, the confluent dripping of the face. The cheeks are a slide from the brows into the valley of the face . . .Each rounded lobe of the vegetable leaf, too, is a thick and now loitering drop . . .!"

When the mercury dives below zero, window frost sprouts and twines as if by fission, upstarting a miniature coal forest of tree forms, fern forms, flower forms, mosses and lichens. And when it melts, you have, if you wish, Henry David's oozing veins and frozen

A frosted window in Madison—Bruce Fritz

The Eau Claire River, Marathon County—Tom Algire

Fractured ice on Lake Superior—Tom Algire

Icicles on red osier dogwood—
Stephen J. Krasemann

fingertips.

In the city, of course, ice is a nasty that blinds car windows, clogs keyholes, sticks doors, spins wheels, slicks sidewalks, and, during the torrents of spring, slides from high roofs in murderous missiles. (Beware in March the old City Hall and the Milwaukee Auditorium.)

Except on skating rinks, the best that can be said for it is that, like snow and rain, it is an irresistible wild invader—one that in an hour can glaze the drabbest downtown street with the sparkling lights of an ice palace. Gone are the days when the unstained icicle offered children nature's own Popsicle. Gone, the swarms of sleighs, sleds, and skaters that, in the 1890s, sported on the clear black ice of a Milwaukee River free of pollution's antifreeze.

Black skating ice! So slick and clear that you could see suckers

The 1860s Dells Mill, on Bridge Creek in
Eau Claire County—Ken Dequaine

darting in the current, a swimming
muskrat pausing to breathe from his
exhaled air bubble. (Although nobody
on my river ever accomplished it,
Fur-Fish-Game magazine swore that
you had only to burst the bubble with a
hatchet to bag a $1.50 pelt.)

At night we would set a stinky
carbide trapper's lamp on the ice and
play hockey, then scorch our Nestor
Johnson Speed Kings around a smoky
willow bonfire. We would race in the
dark over the thin, flexing "rubber ice"
until, at a spring-hole, a knee-deep
plunge would bring instant agony.

The "living soul of ice"? Even a kid
could recognize the death crystals
forming in his stiff, clubbed feet as he
stumped up the hill toward the yellow
lights in the oak grove.

Jay Scriba

Ost is ost and vest is vest.

Gammel ost means "old cheese" in Norwegian. Doubtless there are many varieties, but the kind my mother used to make ranks right up there with Brie, Camembert, and all the other soft cheeses of France. Her old cheese was relatively young, I suspect, but smelled so foul that the uninitiated frequently fled from our table. As one tenderfoot put it, he didn't know whether gammel ost's manufacture consisted of "hanging a pail of milk in the outhouse or a pail of manure in the milk house." If one had the fortitude to get past its absolutely incredible aroma, however, this cheese, smeared on hot homemade bread and served up with black coffee, brought each of us to the threshold of Valhalla.

On the farm, gammel ost was a yearly ritual that began on the cold day in January when Pa came home from town with earth-shattering news: "Well, old Pete Johnson agreed to split our wood again this year."

"When's he coming?" asked Ma.

"Middle of next month."

"I guess I'd better get going on a batch of gammel ost tomorrow. Bring extra milk in from chores tonight."

The process was fairly simple, like making spoiled cottage-cheese. Once the curds were cut and cooked, Ma carefully scooped the pearly spheroids into a clean dish-towel, tied it into a hobo sack, and hung it over the single faucet—cold—in our kitchen sink. The faucet was turned on to rinse the curds, then off so they could drain. Once drained, the curds were dumped into a gray-and-blue crock that announced that truly discriminating shoppers "Buy at Bye's Store, Osseo, Wis." The crock was then placed on a pantry shelf, between the tin bucket of Karo syrup and a stack of laundered Pillsbury's Best flour sacks, which waited to be requisitioned as next year's pillowcases.

After a week and a half, the cheese began to "work," and we began to eat. It was still white, like cottage cheese, but rather gooey. The smell was pungent though not bad, reminiscent of old Limburger. By two weeks later, however, the cheese had turned yellow and smelled frightful. And it had begun to move. Every day the little yellow mountain grew imperceptibly smaller in circumference and greater in height. Pa swore that one day—between the last bite of side pork and the first spoonful of homemade pear sauce—he had seen it move with his naked eye.

In west-central Wisconsin near Eleva—Thomas Peters Lake

In its second month, when the cheese turned greenish brown, our family gave up on it and waited for old Pete. The wood-splitter instinctively arrived at the farmstead, double-bitted ax in gnarled fist, just when the gammel ost was à *point,* brown glop, a ferocious testimonial to the durability of the Norse palate. Pete was about seventy-five, but he split wood with the vigor of a teen-ager and with considerably more skill. By midmorning, the shiny pieces of split wood had grown into a little mountain not unlike the one in the gray-and-blue crock.

At table next to Pa, old Pete looked like a British laborer. Winter and summer, his costume was the same: uncreased brown wool trousers, a forty-year-old black "suit coat," a blue chambray work shirt, and, wonder of wonders to us kids, a vest. Pete hurried through the main course, pork chops and peas, using his knife to ingest everything. He'd skillfully maneuver five peas into a row on the knife blade, poke it past a tobacco-stained moustache into his mouth, then plunge the knife into the pound of butter at center table. I was fascinated. Ma was appalled.

For dessert all but Pete had vanilla pudding. For Pete, Ma brought out the crock. The tips of his moustache quivered with anticipation. Into the crock went his knife; out came a blob. In a few minutes the ost hung in festoons from his moustache and chin. "Awwww—dat's gewd stuff," he said, and glanced down to extract a watch from his vest pocket. "Awwww, yimminy cur-ick-ets! I vent and got ost on my west!"

Fifteen minutes later, out behind the house, the double-bitted ax went up, then down, glinting in the cold February sunlight. Our wood-splitter was back on the job—looking forward to supper and another bout with Ma's contribution to the cheese-maker's art.

David Wood

Along Lacy Road, in Dane County—
Karl R. Lechten

The old-time saloon was the poor man's club. Men gathered in the barbershop or sat around the country-store stove to discuss politics, but for good-fellowship, friendliness, and *Gemütlichkeit* they went to the saloon. To it came men from all walks of life. Within its portals a democratic spirit reigned, and all present became equals.

Standing at the bar with one foot on the rail or sitting around tables, little coteries talked companionably of their families and homes and of their work. They drank a little beer, ate of the free lunch, and then went home or back to their work. Social life today offers few meeting places like the old German saloon. Compared with it, the modern tavern is an arrogant pretender.

Beer had become a favorite American beverage before the close of the Civil War. It had been introduced by the pioneers of German stock who could not accustom themselves to the hard liquors imbibed by some of the other races. With the increase of Teutonic immigration the drinking of beer became a social custom, the saloon a community center. Wherever a goodly number of Germans settled, there a brewery was likely to be established. The ease with which hops and barley could be raised on Wisconsin soil was an important factor in the growth of the industry.

Milwaukee became the chief center of manufacture. . . .Such an impetus did the manufacture of beer receive in Milwaukee that the names of some of its leading brewers continue to be recognized trademarks of our own generation: Captain Frederick Pabst, Joseph Schlitz, Valentin Blatz, and Adam Gettelman. Custom, fashion, and price combined to make it more respectable to drink beer than hard liquor. Not until the bootleg era of prohibition was the public taste for the lighter beverage to wane and the saloon to disappear, probably forever. Today's "tavern" bears so little resemblance to the saloon that it can scarcely be said to be a direct descendant.

. . .the saloon's clientele was not drawn from the highbrow or social-register classes. Nor was its locale confined to Milwaukee. Every city in the state from Superior to Kenosha, from Green Bay to La Crosse, had such gathering places. . . .The saloon supplied the beer which mellowed the discussion of personal, family, state, and national problems. For the price of a nickel one could get a big glass of beer and a substantial lunch and stay as long as he liked. Neighborhood saloonkeepers were usually assisted by their wives and daughters, and before long the men began to be joined at their impromptu club by their wives and other feminine members of the family. When this became common a "Family Entrance" to the saloon was provided. This innovation greatly interested visitors from other cities and gave Milwaukee its reputation as the only American city that welcomed housewives to its saloons. It was often remarked that their presence had a salutary effect on the deportment of their menfolk.

Fred L. Holmes

The Old Spring Tavern, built in 1854, a social center in early Madison—Ken Dequaine

The rise of Milwaukee's distinctive brand of Socialism can be traced back at least to the 1870s, when a workingmen's association founded by Karl Marx in London ten years earlier had a branch in Milwaukee. In 1876, the Social Democrats elected two aldermen. In 1888, a wing of the labor movement led by Paul Grottkau, editor of the *Arbeiter Zeitung*, put up Colin Campbell for mayor on the Socialist Labor ticket. Campbell came out for a number of radical proposals, including abolition of child labor, an eight-hour day on public works projects, and installation of street lights in poor neighborhoods instead of putting them only in rich ones.

It was obvious that a man with such far-out ideas had no chance to be mayor, but a few years later, along came David S. Rose, whose free-and-easy attitude toward prostitution, gambling, and other indoor sports was combined with a talent for winning votes. Mayor Rose's regime made reform almost inevitable, but it was fun while it lasted and kept Socialism at bay a few years longer.

Mayor Rose was in office in 1898 when the Wisconsin Legislature violated a long-standing custom by temporarily raising the beer tax from $1 a barrel to $2. The legislators had a good excuse—there was a war on. The conflict with Spain over Cuba lasted less than four months and most Milwaukeeans who volunteered to fight never got a chance to shoot anybody, but it was felt that paying more for beer was sacrifice enough. The $1 increase in taxes led to a $2 increase in prices as the breweries made sure saloon patrons would get angry enough to do their full part in whipping the Spaniards.

Rose stayed in office until 1906 despite the growing strength of the Socialists and charges by the Republicans that a "brigade of grafters now have Milwaukee by the throat." When Victor Berger ran for mayor in 1904 he claimed that Rose had been

Lake Michigan and the Milwaukee lakefront—
Jerry Kiesow

able to save $150,000 out of his $4,000 salary, a remarkable example of Milwaukee thrift that aroused the Socialist editor's suspicions.

By the time Rose was ready to run for a fifth term, however, he was in trouble. He was charged with spending more time at his silver mine in Arizona than at City Hall. There were rumors involving the mayor and a former Milwaukee woman. Worst of all, he had neglected to put anyone with a Polish name on his ticket. The Republican candidate, Sherburn M. Becker, was only twenty-nine years old but understood that one function of a Milwaukee mayor is to entertain the voters. Becker hired a press agent, organized thirty-five hundred young men into clubs to back his candidacy and offered a barrel of flour to the woman who came up with the best answer to the question of why he should be elected. Meanwhile, William A. Arnold was carrying the Socialist banner, assisted by what the *Sentinel* called "Socialistic slangwhangers from Chicago" who had come north to criticize Milwaukee morals. The Socialists elected eleven aldermen but being accused of associating with Chicagoans was too great a burden for Arnold, who went down to defeat.

So did Mayor Rose, who'd been so confident of winning that he'd left for his mine in Twin Buttes, Arizona, before the votes were counted. Becker took over the mayor's office and thoroughly enjoyed it. He bought a $3,800 crimson-colored Pope-Toledo at a time when some communities still banned horseless carriages from their streets. He got his name in papers coast-to-coast when he set off for Manhattan in his "Red Devil," flying a banner identifying the driver as SHERBURN M. BECKER, BOY MAYOR OF MILWAUKEE.

Becker returned home eventually and continued to make headlines. The Milwaukee *Journal* added a second City Hall reporter and a stenographer to keep up with him. The city attorney hired three additional assistants to defend suits brought against the city. The Boy Mayor might have had a long career ahead of him if he'd been a Democrat. But he was a Republican and the party's leaders felt he was too undignified. They put up Thomas J. Pringle as their candidate in 1908 and Becker's City Hall career was finished. Pringle managed to come in third, behind Emil Seidel and Rose, who went back into office with what he considered a mandate to keep Milwaukee a swinging city.

By now, under Victor Berger's leadership, the Socialist party had moved toward what its critics called "sewer Socialism." There was less emphasis on philosophy and more on the practical housekeeping problems of running a city. The Socialists had fewer than three thousand members, but the party inherited the support of a considerable portion of the labor movement along with a German reform tradition that went all the way back to the Forty-eighters.

Besides, it was time for Rose to be booted out. The voters had tried Becker, only to have his own party repudiate him. In 1910, they decided to see what would happen if they made Emil Seidel, a soft-spoken woodcarver, mayor. Sure, Old Emil was a Socialist. But he was a good German, too, not the sort of fellow who'd go running off to Arizona to speculate in silver. So they voted him into office—the first Socialist ever elected mayor of a large American city. While they were about it, they elected Daniel Webster Hoan city attorney, Carl P. Dietz comptroller, Charles B. Whitnall city treasurer—Socialists, every one of them—and gave the mayor a majority of Socialist aldermen. Melms became the new council president and arrived at his first meeting in a pair of baseball shoes, the only shoes he owned.

The fall of that year, Milwaukeeans gave the Socialists a majority of the board of county supervisors, twelve state assemblymen and the party's first

Milwaukee's last steam-powered tugboat, at Jones Island—Ted Laatsch

congressman, Berger.

Outside of Wisconsin, it was supposed that Milwaukee had gone Marxist. An alderman attending a convention in Indiana had to register in red ink. When Berger went to Washington, he was looked on as a dangerous radical, although it was hard to consider him a menace after people heard his rich Milwaukee accent and listened to his jokes about the trouble he said he was having getting unanimous agreement on policy at the one-man caucus of the Socialist congressional delegation.

Carl Sandburg, a young fellow with a big future ahead, had quit his job as a Milwaukee reporter to be Seidel's secretary. Over steins of beer at Doerfler's Saloon, the Socialists talked of how the local victory could lead to bigger things. The party could go on to win the governorship, perhaps even the presidency. It already had an able candidate in Eugene V. Debs, who had been a labor leader when Berger went to see him in an Illinois jail and recruited him to Socialism.

Seidel lasted for only one term, but Hoan won re-election as city attorney and in 1916 he was elected mayor, an office he held for an unprecedented twenty-four years. By the time he first took office as mayor, however, his party was heading for a crisis over the war. The Socialists were against militarism, and in Milwaukee, at least, this philosophy was complicated by sentimental ties to Germany. By 1918, Debs was in jail and Berger was indicted for violation of the espionage act because of anti-war articles in his newspaper. Milwaukee's Germanic north side sent him back to Congress anyway. Congress wouldn't let him take his seat. Judge Kenesaw Mountain Landis, who had not yet taken up baseball, sentenced him to twenty years in the penitentiary. Berger appealed, campaigned for Congress, and once more, as in 1920, the Milwaukee voters re-elected him. Landis' decision was overruled by the Supreme Court, and Berger served in Congress until 1928.

Whitnall, one of those who triumphed with Seidel in 1910, went on to become the leading spirit in developing Milwaukee County's admirable park system. Hoan kept running and winning until he was beaten in 1940 by a colorful young man named Carl Zeidler, whose brother, Frank, later became Milwaukee's last Socialist mayor, perhaps for all time.

Robert W. Wells

The inhabitants of this region are in the same position as the crew of a ship caught in the ice of the polar seas and forced to hibernate. Their winter is terrible. The temperature remains at 4 degrees below zero; often it lowers to the freezing point of mercury. The lake is covered with a very thick layer of ice, increased further by heavy snowfalls. Often, terrifying storms break the ice crust; the stormy lake piles up the ruins of its prison on the shores and transforms the relief of the coastline overnight. Then the sun pierces through the glacial atmosphere covering the lake; it shines over snow-covered and ice-covered mountains.

Camille Pisani

A water-hollowed cave in the Apostle Islands—Tom Algire

Following spread:
Frozen Lake Superior at Squaw Bay, in the Apostle Islands National Lakeshore—Tom Algire

Sunrise at the Kewaunee harbor, at 5 degrees below zero—Jon T. Wildgrube

154

At Storr's Lake Wildlife Area, just outside Milton, in Rock County—Gary Garnett

It starts out as a hunt—
the elusive cottontail our quarry,
hasenpfeffer our objective.
But first a cup of coffee
slurped with hurried discomfort,
the rest placed in a plastic thermos
that ought to melt but doesn't.
Next insulated boots
that smell of neat's-foot oil,
fitted firmly over red wool socks
that stained two T-shirts
in the wash, oh well.
Then a quiet walk to Simpson's Pond.
Harold, the beagle, house pet
turned firebrand for the occasion,
acts as his own snowplow,
meandering nose-down, tail-up
through last night's gift of snow.
The sun foretells its presence
with a yellow, then red,
then orange iridescence to our left.

No clouds to hold what little heat
the sun will have to offer.
Our paths and Harold's furrow
cross telltale tracks
of curious lagomorphs
perhaps seeking buried grasses
perhaps companionship
perhaps both.
The guttural euphony of a narrow creek
feeding the pond is our welcome,
and almost simultaneously
the sun sends irregular lines of light
through the naked oaks
forming a corridor to denser thickets
and our destination.
Tracks become more numerous,
their recent origin confirmed
by Harold's tail sweeping to and fro
like a cat-o'-nine-tails
in the grasp of an enraged
schoolmarm.
Light filters through the gnarled arms
of aged trees and off a zillion or two

Along Carter Creek two miles west of Friendship,
in Adams County—George G. Mock, III

A northern lake in winter—Brian Milne

white hexagonal edges.
The sun floats cautiously
into visibility from the east,
where we knew it would.
Harold sings as only Harold can
and lurches off in pursuit
of the as yet unseen rabbit.
It suddenly appears
and the two begin a chase
that is as old and predictable
as rabbits and beagles themselves.
Into the woods and gone
except for Harold's comic opera,
his effort to keep us informed
of their progress and his tenacity.
As the song becomes more distant
we relax,
knowing we have discovered an animal
of considerable territorial range—
Harold never was particularly selective.
Our attention is focused on the pond
and we are taken aback
by the winter spectacle.
Low bushes are covered with hundreds
of brilliant, frozen crystals
brighter than any usual gem.
A breeze, as if for our benefit,
scatters shards of resplendent jewelry
onto a fragile film of ice
that partially covers the pond.
We observe a single feather
buoyed against the brilliant blue
of winter water,
the remnant of a dawdling mallard
forced at last to find the warmth
of lower latitudes.
Our gaze shifts to tufts of reed canary
adorned in hoarfrost, a foreign hue
in the white-blue tapestry
of the winter landscape.
Ours are the eyes of the beholder
perceiving the seasonal posture
of this not uncommon place,
sensing a sort of tranquillity
that is more easily felt than described.
Where were we during winters past?
Muffled sounds of our trustworthy dog
remind us of our mission,
but a catharsis of an intriguing nature
has voided thoughts of guns
and strategy and hasenpfeffer.
Harold appears
several seconds behind
a probably confused rabbit,
who is wondering, if rabbits do,
why that raucous beast won't quit.
It scampers by only yards away
and neither gun is raised.
Sorry, Harold, not today.
We found something else to take home
this morning forever.

Richard McCabe

The land lies sleeping
in the snow.
The farm now warm
and tight and snug.
Feather ticks
and ticking clocks.
A blue spruce tree
and Christmas socks.
Rich fruitcake
and fat rum balls.
A piny smell
all through the halls.
Mama in the kitchen,
the big cats too.
The kids and the kittens
go chasing a shoe.
In the brush piles, the rabbits—
hutched up and spare.
Watching for weasels
and waiting
for spring.

George Vukelich

Near Marxville, in Dane County—Ken Dequaine

Credits